Group's εmεrgεncy Rεsponsε
handbook
for: YOUTH MINISTRY

D1115964

Loveland, Colorado
www.group.com

Group's Emergency Response Handbook for Youth Ministry

Copyright © 2007 Group Publishing, Inc.

Visit our Web site: **www.group.com**

Credits
Contributors: Brian Diede, Jeremy Holburn, Joy-Elizabeth F. Lawrence, James W. Miller, Siv M. Ricketts, Summer Rivers Salomonsen, Christina Schofield, and Fred Whaples
Editor: Janna Kinner
Project Manager: Amber Van Schooneveld
Senior Developer: Roxanne Wieman
Copy Editor: Daniel Birks
Chief Creative Officer: Joani Schultz
Book Designer/Print Production Artist: Pamela Poll Graphic Design
Cover Art Director/Designer: Jeff A. Storm
Illustrator: Pamela Poll
Production Manager: DeAnne Lear

Unless otherwise indicated, all Scripture quotations are taken from the *Holy Bible*, New Living Translation, copyright © 1996, 2004. Used by permission of Tyndale House Publishers, Inc., Wheaton, IL 60189. All rights reserved.

Library of Congress Cataloging-in-Publication Data

Group's emergency response handbook for youth ministry. – 1st American
pbk. ed.
    p. cm.
  Includes bibliographical references.
  ISBN 978-0-7644-3574-4 (pbk. : alk. paper)
 1. Church work with youth. 2. Crisis management–Religious
aspects–Christianity. 3. Crisis intervention (Mental health services)
4. Pastoral psychology. I. Group Publishing.

  BV4447.G697 2007
  259'.23–dc22

                                              2007008799

10 9 8 7 6 5 4 3   16 15 14 13 12 11 10 09 08 07

Printed in the United States of America.

Contents

Introduction

It's not easy losing a parent. Or dealing with depression. Or facing an addiction. It's hard and painful and brutal.

But it doesn't have to be lonely.

Christians should never have to face trials on their own, especially teenagers. Those around them—their Christian brothers and sisters—should rise up and support them.

"Share each other's burdens, and in this way obey the law of Christ" (Galatians 6:2).

Although it isn't easy going through trials, it's also tough being on the outside and trying to help teenagers in your ministry who are suffering.

You don't know what to do. You're worried about hurting their feelings or stepping on their toes or saying the exact *wrong* thing.

Of course you care—you love them! It isn't that you don't want to help—it's just that you don't know how.

Group's Emergency Response Handbook for Youth Ministry will help you come alongside those in your youth group who are facing tough times. From care and counseling tips, to practical ideas for your group, to what to say and what not to say, this book offers insight after insight into how to care for the hurting in your youth group.

Of course, it'd be great if you never had to pick up this book! But the reality is that everyone faces tough times—including the teenagers and families in your youth ministry. And they need your help.

So when someone you love is going through the pain of parents divorcing, dealing with an eating disorder, or considering suicide…it's time to pick up this guide. Use the Table of Contents to find the specific hurt you're concerned about, and then flip to that section.

Once there, you'll find a **real-life narrative**—a story from someone who's been there. Sometimes they're inspiring, and you'll read how the support and love of a youth group sustained someone through a hard time. Other times they're disappointing and tell stories of people left alone during tragedy or rejected during trial. Either way, these stories will move you, and they'll show you the importance of devoted youth ministers.

Each section also includes **care and counseling tips** that will give you practical ideas for reaching out in love. From listening to youth, to mediating in arguments, to intentional reminiscing, these ideas will help you effectively support the hurting people in your small group.

Next, you'll find **group tips** for your whole youth group. These practical ideas will help your entire group support the hurting member during his or her trial.

And finally, you'll find an invaluable section on **what to say and what not to say** to your friend. The words we use can help or hurt a student more than we know. This section will help you avoid the hurtful comments and use the helpful ones.

You'll also find useful boxes in each section that offer Scripture help, guidelines for referring your student to a professional counselor, and additional resources, such as books and Web sites, that you can use as you support your hurting teenager. This book is your guide for help in a crisis, but it doesn't take the place of legal or medical advice. You may need to seek professional help or the advice of your pastor in some situations.

Our prayer for this book is that it will help you help a student during a difficult time.

"He comforts us in all our troubles so that we can comfort others. When they are troubled, we will be able to give them the same comfort God has given us" (2 Corinthians 1:4).

CHAPTER ONE

Grief
Supporting Students During Loss

with counseling insights from **JULIA A. ODELL, M.A.**
+ ministry tips from **SIV M. RICKETTS**

Dear Diary,

It's been three weeks and two days since Dad died, and this is the first time I've felt like writing. I'm not even sure why I feel like writing now, but maybe it's that some of the shock has worn off and enough grief has bubbled up to the surface that I have to get it out somewhere. At least I'm able to cry now. I heard a neighbor's child crying the day after Dad died, and I almost felt jealous. I wished I could just bawl like a baby, but the tears wouldn't come. Here they are…

I feel like someone has lopped off a part of my heart and there's no one to talk to. Most people really don't want to hear all this. Oh, sure, they might listen, but then I don't want to burden anyone. My friends put up with so much from me during Dad's illness that I think they've gotten bored, if not with me then at least with this situation. Now that he's gone, and especially now that some time has passed, they seem to think that life can go back to normal. Sorry—I don't know what "normal" is anymore. I guess they just don't know what to say, so they want to ignore it. If only…

I went to church this morning for the first time since he died. I know I need God, but I'm still so awkward around people. I don't know how to be anymore. I wasn't sure I would go, but then Geary called and asked if he could give me a ride. Of course, I could have driven myself, but like I said, I might not have. It was good to be out with a friend, to have someone to walk in the doors with and to sit next to.

Because I felt out of place, I couldn't sit in my normal spot. It was the first time I've been in a crowd since the memorial service, and most of those people were Mom's friends. And Geary was OK with us bolting as soon as the service was over. I couldn't take the sad glances and well-meaning words—I'm not ready to gracefully receive the condolences of people who don't know me well enough or care enough to come by the house. I'll dissolve into a puddle—so embarrassing for everyone. I hope people will understand that I've been through a lot and still accept me when I'm ready to fully be there again.

I just can't believe Dad's gone. My mind keeps flashing pictures of him at different times: my little sister dancing on his toes, ice cream after school plays, that fancy dinner when I graduated from elementary school, vacation and holiday memories. And then when he got sick. His skin turned an odd yellow-gray color. He walked slowly and hunched over. Dad in the hospital bed. At the end I wanted to believe that maybe we had a few more weeks, but really we had only hours. And then it was a blessing, for him and for all of us, that it didn't go on any longer. But I don't want anyone else to say that. I have to live through this, and I can't take anyone making me feel bad for how I'm dealing with it.

It is interesting how everyone deals with it differently, though. My sister has been able to break the tension and make us laugh at all the right times. My brother has been fascinated by all the medical stuff, and he even was able to comfort Dad sometimes by explaining what was going on. Mom has been quiet, going through the motions. I've been on a rollercoaster—sometimes fine, sometimes a mess, never knowing how I'm going to feel moment by moment.

Oh, Dad, I miss you so much!

You know, Geary was great this morning. In the car he asked if I wanted to talk, so we did some, but then I asked about "the world outside," or at least that's how I'm thinking of it, the world beyond my grief. He told me what's been going on at school and at youth group and shared funny stories about crazy coffee orders he gets at his job in the coffee shop. We laughed and it felt good. I sure haven't laughed much recently. After church we grabbed some food and watched a goofy movie on TV, and then he came with me to walk my dog. It was good just to hang out. With a friend like that, maybe, slowly, I will edge back to a new kind of normal.

When he was leaving Geary asked what he could tell people if they asked how they could help. Tough question. My mom seems to like it that people have brought food. None of us has much of an appetite, but four small appetites still add up to more cooking than Mom has the energy to satisfy. I think she also appreciates seeing people without having to put out effort. People come over, bring food, chat for a while, and then leave. Sometimes they pray with her, or with us, and that can be nice. I guess it depends on how comfortable they are. If they feel awkward talking about death, then their prayers sound even more awkward. But some people must have a gift of prayer because during and after I feel better, more hopeful, like they tore a hole in our roof so God could pour himself down on us.

But what kind of help do I need? What I don't want is for people to assume they know how I feel, or to tell me how I should feel, or to assume they know what I need or will make me feel better. I'd like to get off this rollercoaster more than anyone would like to see me get off this roller-coaster, but for now, this is where I am. That has to be OK.

Sometimes I wish people would just come over and hang out without asking me too many questions. Other times I wish they'd listen. Or I guess people could help me get motivated in general, like offering to go to the library and study together, even if we studied different things. Or, like Geary did, come with me to walk my dog. My poor dog has spent too much time in the yard lately. And I used to have a list of chores...OK, I know no one really wants to do chores with me, but still, they would go faster doing them together, and the yard is looking a little shabby.

The best help would be that, whatever someone did or said, they did or said it with love. I've lost a huge source of love. No one can ever replace Dad, and no one will ever love me with the same kind of love he had for me. But to know that I am loved—that there are people in my life who will stand by me, listen to me, pray for me, and support me in ways I can hear, see, and feel...that I'm not forgotten—that would be huge.

Care and Counseling Tips

THE BASICS

Many of your students will experience the death of a parent, relative, or friend during their teenage years. As a youth leader, you can help support them by learning about the process they are going through.

+ Grief has predictable stages.

The many stages of grief include shock or denial (this isn't happening to me), anger (why is this happening to me?), guilt (it's my fault), bargaining (I'll be a better person if…), sadness or depression (I don't care anymore), and acceptance (I'm ready for whatever comes next). Denial is a normal coping mechanism that protects the individual from experiencing a flood of emotions too quickly. If a student instantly realized and accepted the full reality of a loved one's death, with all the ramifications, he or she would be overwhelmed. However, by accepting the loss in bits and pieces, the individual can deal with it slowly.

+ Grieving is different for each individual.

The grief process will look different for each student. Once a student begins to *feel* his or her emotions, he or she will not progress through the stages of grief in a linear fashion, by completing one stage and moving to the next. Instead, a grieving person typically cycles through the stages, making it possible to experience anger one day (or even one hour) and sadness the next. It is crucial that you allow a person to experience and work through *each* of the stages and emotions.

The intensity and duration of grief will vary depending on factors such as the type of loss, an individual's coping skills, previous experiences, and the available resources to support them.

Care Tips

While supporting your grieving teenagers will require a long-term commitment from you, there are some immediate things you can do to help.

+ Listen.

The most beneficial thing that you can do for a grieving teenager is to be a good listener. The bereaved student will need a safe place to share feelings and thoughts. Being a good listener requires time and energy. Grieving individuals may want to talk about the deceased incessantly, often repeating stories and memories. While listening, don't give advice until asked for input.

+ Normalize the student's feelings.

You can help your grieving student see that any feelings he or she has about the loss are normal. Don't place expectations on how the student should feel—any feeling is normal and should be accepted. If your student shares that he or she has been feeling sad or guilty about the death, even a simple "That sounds pretty normal" can go a long way in helping the student feel that he or she is not crazy or alone.

+ Allow normal activities to continue.

As soon as possible after a death, reintroduce activities into the student's life, such as encouraging him or her to get back into your youth group meetings or events. Getting back to some normalcy will help your student realize that other parts of life can feel normal again, too, and will help him or her avoid slipping into isolation or depression.

+ Don't forget about the family.

The loss has likely had an impact on the student's parents, siblings, and extended family members as well. This is a great time for you to build a supportive relationship with the family by checking in and seeing how you can be helpful. There are often practical things that you can organize your youth group to do, such as house-sitting during a funeral, gardening, or preparing meals.

WHEN TO REFER

If a student exhibits the following behaviors, a referral to a professional Christian counselor or psychologist is recommended:

+ **The student is unwilling or unable to talk to anyone about his or her feelings about the death.**
+ **The student's eating or sleeping patterns have significantly changed since the loss and are disrupting daily functioning.**
+ **The student is using drugs, alcohol, food, or sex to cope with the loss.**
+ **The student has withdrawn to the point of completely isolating him or herself from friends or family.**
+ **The student appears to be stuck in one of the grief stages, and you have exhausted your time and emotional resources in trying to help.**

Counseling Tips

The initial crisis of the loss will pass with time, but the grief process may take awhile. Continue supporting your grieving students in these ways:

✦ Encourage the expression of feelings.

As time passes, continue to facilitate the expression of the student's feelings by asking open-ended questions about the deceased person, such as:

- What's your favorite memory with [the deceased loved one]?
- Which quality did you most appreciate about him [her], and why?
- What would you most like to tell him or her?

Writing in a journal is an effective way for a teenager to express and work through feelings individually. You can encourage the student to write in the journal before bed each night, to recap the events of the day and to identify the various emotions that the student experienced. A teenager can read his or her journal entries with a friend or support person, or he or she may decide to keep the journal private.

✦ Participate in therapeutic activities.

You can also participate in therapeutic activities with the student. Asking him or her to show and discuss pictures of the deceased is an easy way to facilitate the process of grieving. Other activities symbolize letting go, such as sending a toy boat down a river together or releasing balloons into the air. It may be helpful for the bereaved person to write a goodbye letter first and then attach the letter to the boat or balloons. You may wish to pray aloud or read a Scripture passage, such as Psalm 121, before releasing the symbolic item.

Students can express anger through safe physical activities such as punching a punching bag, screaming into a pillow, ripping up pieces of paper, or throwing rocks into a lake. These are helpful because they allow students to release physical energy and express frustration and anger in ways that do not cause harm to themselves, others, or valuable property.

+ Take care of yourself.

Ministering to someone who has recently lost a loved one can be physically, emotionally, and spiritually draining. Developing a support system is critical. Don't consider yourself the only support for the student: Actively seek out friends and family who are available for support. You might suggest that other adults or students call and check in with the student.

SCRIPTURE HELP

+ **Psalm 23**
+ **Psalm 31:9, 14**
+ **Psalm 139:13-16**
+ **Lamentations 3:31-33**
+ **John 11:17-44**

+ **Romans 5:1-5**
+ **Romans 8:35-39**
+ **2 Corinthians 4:6-12**
+ **Philippians 3:10-14**
+ **1 Peter 1:3-4**

Group Tips

+ Go to church together.
Offer to give the mourner a ride. Getting out the door can be a difficult step for someone who is grieving. Knowing he or she doesn't have to make the effort alone can be a tremendous support.

+ Remember important dates.
Organize your group to call or write a card every week for the first month and then every month for at least six months. Also remember the mourner on special days like holidays, birthdays, and the anniversary of the death. He or she needs tangible remembrances of your love and support long after the first few weeks. Grief comes in waves and often feels more intense just when one might expect it to lessen.

+ Pray together.
Shower grieving students in prayer, gently reminding them of the One who knows them better than they know themselves, who loves them, who will always be with them, and who offers hope for today and tomorrow.

What Not to Say

+ "I know just how you feel."
Grieving is such an intensely personal process that you have no idea how someone feels, even if you are grieving yourself. The mourner may not be sure how he or she feels from moment to moment, so you can't assume you know. Allow time and space for the mourner to share with you how he or she feels during the process.

+ "They're better off."
It may be true but still don't say it. The mourner can say it, but if you say it, it can sound like an invalidation of the person's feelings of loss and grief and worse, an accusation of selfishness.

+ "They'll always be in your heart."
Of course, the mourner will always have memories, but right now they'd rather have the flesh-and-blood person.

What to Say

+ "I don't know what to say."
Grief can make even the most confident speaker feel awkward, so if you don't know what to say, just admit it. Honesty is refreshing.

+ "Do you want to talk about it?"
Sometimes it helps to talk, and other times silence helps most. Sometimes mourners want to look through photo albums and share memories; other times they want to be distracted with chitchat about almost anything else.

+ "Do you know how I can best help you?"
In the past your student might have really loved cornball movies but now

might prefer going for a walk. The student might like to go on as if nothing has happened or might like you to help the world "stop" for a time (collecting homework assignments or taking his or her baby-sitting jobs for a while) so the student can just live this time of grief. He or she may not even know the kind of help needed; in that case, check back in a few days or a week and see if your student has thought of something specific you can do to help.

ADDITIONAL RESOURCES

+ Books

Don't Ask for the Dead Man's Golf Clubs: What to Do and Say (And Not to) When a Friend Loses A Love One. Lynn Kelly. New York: Workman Publishing Company, Inc., 2000.

The Grieving Teen: A Guide for Teenagers and Their Friends. Helen Fitzgerald. New York: Simon & Schuster, 2000.

+ Online Resources

www.griefnet.org (GriefNet)
www.helpguide.org (Helpguide)
www.hospicenet.org (Hospice)

CHAPTER TWO

Depression

Supporting Your Teenager in the Darkness

with counseling insights from
REBEKAH KNIGHT-BAUGHMAN, PH.D.
+ ministry tips from **SIV M. RICKETTS**

Cleo is an 18-year-old high school senior. She has been dealing with depression as long as she can remember.

Emergency Response Handbook: *How did you first know you were depressed?*

Cleo: I didn't. I thought I was normal, that everyone felt that way. I don't remember a time in my life when I didn't feel depressed. I never had much self-confidence, and I was an easy target for others to pick on—especially those people I thought were my friends. They would tell me their secrets because I could always keep a secret, but they wouldn't return the favor. My secrets became the brunt of jokes around school. But they were my friends so I just took it. They laughed but then they'd call me later. I didn't know any better.

Eventually, people began to say things like, "You're always so sad." But even then I didn't know. Everyone was depressed, or at least said they were. It was kind of a cool thing to be. Finally, my mom and dad took me to a therapist, who diagnosed me as depressed. Not just sad, but clinically depressed.

ERH: *What's the difference?*

Cleo: Everyone has times in their life when they are sad and usually for a good reason. You start a new school and don't know anyone. Your dog dies. You didn't make the team. You fail a big test that will seriously affect your grade. That kind of thing. Depression can start with a traumatic event, but it doesn't go away. You feel sad long after you should be over it. And depression can be a biological problem where the body doesn't regulate hormones correctly. Sometimes it takes medication to deal with it.

ERH: *Have you tried medication?*

Cleo: Yup. But the drugs made everything worse, made me crazy. I couldn't sleep more than three hours a night. I talked so fast people couldn't understand me. I seriously thought I was going out of my mind. So in my case, my doctor pulled me off drugs.

ERH: *So no meds. How about therapy?*

Cleo: Well, I've had good therapists but mostly bad ones. One talked to me like I was 4 years old. He wanted me to pull questions from his "Bear's Jar of Questions" in order to give us a topic to discuss. Seriously, I was in junior high! I know others who are in therapy, and they say it works for them. Mostly I've tried to find other ways to cope.

ERH: *Like what?*

Cleo: Exercise is the best. It naturally raises your endorphin levels, which makes you feel good. It's hard to get started (OK, you think it's hard for you, but when you're depressed, you just want to sleep all the time!), but even one workout can make me feel so much better. And when I work out regularly I sleep better, too, which helps everything.

Oh, and my church. My church makes me want to move, to do stuff. My church is the best thing for me. I am so grateful that God brought me to this great church. I can't even really explain it to you, but I love it.

ERH: *OK, let's go back. Can you describe what depression feels like?*

Cleo: I think everyone has some idea, but how's this: Take your sad memories, multiply them, and then drag them out over the rest of your life. Depression makes you not want to do anything—no friends, no sports, nothing you enjoyed before. You feel lethargic. You just want to sleep and be alone. You get irritated when you have to interact with the world or when things aren't the way you want them. You know sometimes in cartoons or commercials a little black rain cloud follows someone around dumping on them all the time? That's how it feels. You're dark and stormy and wet and grumpy about it.

ERH: *How did others respond to your depression?*

Cleo: Oh, people give up. They don't notice or if they notice they don't do anything about it. They let you fall and that's the worst. I had friends but they got busy. Maybe they thought I was busy, too, but I wasn't and they would have known that if they'd called. But then it's hard to acknowledge something's going on, so they'd put off calling, thinking they'd call later or tomorrow or on the weekend, and time passes and they don't.

Teachers, who you'd think should notice, would blame laziness. One particularly bad time my freshman year of high school I could barely drag myself to classes, and sometimes I just didn't go. One of my friends decided, without telling me, that he would do my class project for me. He knew in my state I wasn't going to get it done, so he worked extra hard to finish his early, and then he did mine. I wasn't in class that day, so I didn't even know about it until it was done. He did such a great job. It was beautiful and so artistic and the teacher should have known there was no possible way I could have done it, but she didn't. I don't recommend it, I know it seems bad, but that was a huge help. Maybe he didn't handle it the "right" way, but my friend totally demonstrated that he cared about me.

ERH: *Did other friends respond well?*

Cleo: I have one friend who, when things get bad, will call me every night at bedtime to see if I'm tired enough to sleep, and if not, she'll talk with me until I can. I have another friend who calls every other Thursday to make plans for the weekend. They're great. I know I can count on them, that they'll be there for me when I need them most.

ERH: *Anything else you want people to know?*

Cleo: Depression is not the end of the world. Sure, sometimes it feels like it, but you can go on. There are ways to deal with it, whether you get therapy, medication, handle it with the help of family and friends, or all of the above. Depression is part of who I am. Oh, when I think about it, I wish I wasn't depressed, but hey, what doesn't kill you makes you stronger, right? You just have to be honest with yourself and others. Watch yourself. Set good boundaries. Be healthy. And do what you can to enjoy life.

SCRIPTURE HELP

+ **2 Samuel 22:7**
+ **Psalm 42:1-8**
+ **Psalm 107:13-15**
+ **Psalm 121**
+ **Isaiah 40:27-31**

+ **Jeremiah 29:11**
+ **Lamentations 3:21-26**
+ **Romans 5:1-8**
+ **Romans 12:12**
+ **1 Peter 1:3-9**

MEDICATION

Many mental health professionals agree that medication in conjunction with therapy can help those suffering from severe depression. Encourage your student's parents to openly discuss with their psychiatrist any questions or concerns they may have.

Care and Counseling Tips

THE BASICS

Depression is a dark and oppressive mood problem that can feel unbearable to the student suffering from it. The burden of depression drags the person down as he or she tries to carry on with life as usual when life is not "as usual." Yet there is hope. By understanding the basic symptoms and causes for depression and learning to express care in ways that the teenager who is depressed will receive well, you can share the burden of depression with your student, and he or she will begin to feel the weight of depression lift. Look for the following symptoms if you think a student may be depressed:

+ Emotional Symptoms: hopelessness, sadness, discouragement, anxiety, irritability, frequent crying, sharp and hurtful comments, a pessimistic outlook, feeling overwhelmed by life

+ Physical Symptoms: change in appetite and in sleep patterns, physical complaints, taking more trips to the doctor than usual, decreased energy, tiredness, fatigue

+ Cognitive Symptoms: thinking negatively about him or herself, making self-deprecating comments, difficulty thinking clearly, difficulty concentrating, inability to make decisions, thoughts of death

+ Behavioral Symptoms: decline in personal hygiene, change in sleeping habits, inability to enjoy things he or she normally loves

+ Spiritual Symptoms: difficulty connecting with God and believing in God's goodness, difficulty praying, feeling hopeless or guilty

+ Reasons for Depression

Most mental health practitioners agree that a combination of internal and external factors affect a person's mood. Here are some common influencers of depression:

- Genetic, biochemical, and hormonal factors
- Family history of depression
- Losing a relationship (death or breakup)
- Feeling unsafe and insecure
- Moving or changing schools
- Negative thinking
- Isolation

WHEN TO REFER

Clinical depression is a debilitating illness that can be life-threatening. It's one of the most common mental health problems, but it often goes unrecognized, especially in adolescents. Make a referral to a professional Christian counselor, psychologist, or psychiatrist when

+ Your student is at risk of hurting him or herself.

If your student expresses a desire to end his or her life, get help. Call 911 for immediate assistance. (See Chapter 3, "Suicide," for a list of risk factors.)

+ Your student is a danger to others.

If your student expresses a desire to harm another person, refer him or her to a mental health care worker, and notify the person whom he or she has plans to harm.

+ The student's daily functioning is impaired.

If the student is unable to get out of bed, eat, or groom or bathe, get help.

Care Tips

You can join with your student in planning and carrying out goals that will help move him or her along the road toward wellness. This role must be approached with caution, however, because it's difficult for a person who is not depressed to understand how debilitating the illness really is. For those who are depressed, it can be hard to find energy for even a small task that seems easy to you—even making a phone call to a friend or taking a walk around the block can seem like impossible assignments. Keeping that in mind, here are some tips for helping and understanding your student with depression:

+ Actively listen.
Encouraging your student to talk about his or her sadness will foster understanding, which can help the person feel a sense of control over his or her emotions instead of feeling controlled by them.

+ Take the student seriously.
Don't minimize the situation. You can validate your student's emotions by expressing understanding and care. Normalizing depression can also help the person feel less alone in the process.

+ Get on a schedule.
People with depression often have problems with sleeping (too much or too little) and eating (loss of appetite or overeating). Encourage your student to stick to a consistent bedtime every night and a healthy eating schedule. Being in a routine will help him or her get back on track.

+ Be nonjudgmental.
People with depression judge themselves every day, so the last thing they need is a youth leader who judges them, too. Communicate patience and grace. By doing this, you may help them become more patient and gracious toward themselves.

Counseling Tips

Many times, depression calls for a professional counselor. Even so, there are many ways you can personally help counsel your student through this tough time.

+ Build and maintain trust.

Trust takes time—it takes positive experiences built on more positive experiences. But once trust is built, it's easy to break—especially when things said in confidence are shared later with others. Be clear with your students about your policy of confidentiality—they should know upfront that you can't keep a secret if they disclose they might hurt themselves or someone else.

+ Challenge faulty thinking.

Depression impairs people's thinking. People with depression often feel unworthy of good relationships, doing well in school, or feeling a close connection with God. Help your student understand that recovery from depression is a process and that he or she is deserving of healthy relationships with others and God and a promising future.

+ Create positive affirmations.

Low self-esteem can be an issue for many adolescents, but especially for teenagers experiencing depression. They often can't think of anything positive about themselves. Encourage them to list their positive attributes, and remind them that they are made in God's image.

Group Tips

+ Be consistent.

Few things can be as harmful to those who are depressed as inconsistent friends. Depression often involves low self-esteem, lack of confidence, and negative thinking, all of which are confirmed when the people they thought (or hoped) they could count on don't come through. Encourage group members to pick a time to call their depressed friend and do so every day or every week.

+ Appeal to the senses.

Depression can feel like sitting in a thick fog, and a sensory surprise can help to clear the air. Bring your student a sweet-smelling flower or an aromatic candle (smell), a favorite food (taste), a CD (hearing), a soft stuffed animal or scarf (touch), or a picture of a happy time together (sight). You don't have to spend much except your time and creativity to offer your friend a sweet surprise.

+ No outsiders.

When your friend is in public, make sure he or she is always in the middle of the group. This may sound goofy but it's serious. For example, don't let the depressed student sit at the end of a row at the movies, but make sure he or she has someone on either side. The person at the end can have trouble hearing others' conversations and feel left out. In fact, for someone who's depressed, being with people can make the loneliness even more intense (generating feelings of insecurity or worry that he or she isn't connecting with others), so as a group, make every effort to keep your friend in the center of the action. Just don't be too obvious about it.

What Not to Say

+ "You'll snap out of it."

Sometimes depression is more than just being sad and may require medical intervention. Even once a person is under a doctor's supervision, expect the person to feel better over time, not immediately.

+ "Just think positive."

Positive thinking is a good goal to work toward, but stating it this way can make someone feel as if all his or her concerns and feelings—and maybe his or her life itself—are invalid. Try listening without trying to fix your student's problems.

+ "Don't be so sad. Nothing is all that bad."

Biology, psychology, and environment may all play a role in causing someone to be depressed, so circumstances alone can't always account for it. Negative thinking, including feelings of worthlessness and hopelessness, is part of the depression and not something that you can dismiss. You can, however, gently help your teenager see things from a different perspective.

What to Say

+ "Let's go out."

People who are depressed tend to isolate themselves from family, friends, and the world. Explain to your student that there is a link between being isolated and feeling lonely or depressed. Because of depression, your student lacks motivation and energy to get out on his or her own. Take the initiative to organize an outing your student has enjoyed in the past, and then don't take "no" for an answer.

+ "I'm here for you."

Don't just say it—live it. Be there for your student. Listen when your student wants to talk. Hang out regularly. Initiate activities your student will enjoy. Do what it takes to demonstrate commitment to your group member. It won't always be easy to spend time with a depressed person, but you may be part of God's healing process for him or her.

+ "How can I pray for you?"

God offers hope and love. Even if your student feels like he or she can't pray, you can pray for your student.

ADDITIONAL RESOURCES

+ Books
Feeling Good: The New Mood Therapy. David D. Burns. New York: Avon Books, 1980, 1999.

+ Online Resources
www.nimh.nih.gov/publicat/friend.cfm
(National Institute of Mental Health)

http://www.psychologyinfo.com/depression/teens.htm
(Psychology Information Online)

www.safeyouth.org
(National Youth Violence Prevention Resource Center)

CHAPTER THREE

Suicide
Intervening Before It's Too Late

with counseling insights from **KELLY M. FLANAGAN, PH.D**
+ ministry tips from **FRED WHAPLES**

"I am all alone. No one cares any longer. I have no place to turn. I hate my life and my family, and I have no friends. For those who wonder why, this is all they need to know. I am all alone."

These words of utter despair were written on a three-ring piece of school notebook paper left on the nondescript desk of a teenager whose family were members of my congregation. I had visited the student many times, striving to get to know him, but he pushed me away each time. Billy just refused to let me in.

I remember on one particular occasion I had stopped by the school to have lunch with students in my youth program. I saw Billy across the room, alone as usual. Quiet. Reserved and closed off, if not downright antisocial. I approached Billy, only to be quickly glared at and then told to "leave me alone." Feeling rejected, I gave Billy the space I thought was necessary. That was just 10 days before finding the letter—the letter that devastated a family and changed a youth ministry forever.

Upon discovering the letter, Billy's mom called me and cried out for help. I agreed to meet her and her husband at the school immediately. As I frantically drove that day to the high school, my mind raced with fears and failures. What could I have done? Why didn't I work harder? Why didn't I see this coming? Why…why…why…Then I realized something very important: This wasn't about me—this was about Billy.

I arrived at the school where officials had now detained Billy in a private space with counselors. As I walked into the room, I couldn't help but wonder, What can I say? What can I do? I frantically prayed for guidance.

I waited until Billy's devastated parents arrived. They had so many questions they needed answered but were simply finding no answers. We prayed together in the school office area and proceeded to enter the room where Billy was waiting with a school counselor. Mom rushed to envelop him in a bearhug, while Dad just knelt beside the chair and placed one arm on the back of each member of his distraught family.

The school counselor excused herself, and I moved a couple more chairs into the room. We sat in a circle and began to ask Billy the obvious questions: Why? Why did you feel unloved? Why did you feel so hopeless? Why did you…

Billy began to unravel a hard story. At home, Mom and Dad were fighting more than ever. At school, friends were impossible to make, grades were horrible, and teachers were harsh at times. Even at church, there were far too many cliques and way too many fakes. Billy felt all alone. He had left the letter on the desk with the full intent of never making it home that day.

I reached out to Billy and took his hand in mine. Getting down on one knee in front of him, I began to weep. "Billy, I am sorry that I failed you. You are an amazing young man with so much to offer, but I have been so busy filling my life with other things that I missed you. I have been so busy telling people about this Jesus who heals and helps that I stopped being that Jesus. Billy, will you forgive me? Will you give me another chance? Will you allow me the opportunity to get to know you? Will you give life another chance so that I can see how full it can be with you in it?" At this, Billy began to shed a few tears and agreed to give it one more try.

In the weeks that followed, Billy was placed in professional counseling, which also included daily visits from me. On one particular visit, I was able to pray with Billy as he rededicated his life to Jesus Christ.

Once Billy was released from residential care, I visited him nearly every day and was able to take him along with me as I visited the homes of other students. Billy began to build a network of friends. His parents were now doing family devotions every evening together (the strife and division nearly gone), and he had even joined a school club. Billy now had a reason to live. Life had purpose.

WHEN TO REFER

+ Always!

It's always possible that you've overestimated the person's risk of suicide. However, in this situation, it's better to err on the safe side. You'll rest easier knowing that you've done the best thing possible for the student.

+ Always!

If the risk of suicide seems to be high, you can do several things. First, your student could call the National Suicide Prevention Lifeline (1-800-273-TALK). Second, if the student is unwilling to talk to someone about his or her feelings and plans, you can call 911 for an emergency response team. Finally, if you feel comfortable, you could drive the student to the nearest emergency room for evaluation.

+ Always!

Even if your student seems at low risk for suicide, you should insist on joining him or her in the process of seeking professional intervention. Professionals include psychologists and counselors, suicide prevention centers, a family doctor, or other resources within your church.

Care and Counseling Tips

THE BASICS

As a youth leader, you're unlikely to face anything that frightens you as much as a student who is considering suicide. Ultimately, your job is simple—to persuade the teenager to get professional help. However, reality is often more complex. The first thing to do is learn to detect the presence of suicidal thoughts. Many teenagers will directly tell you that they're thinking about suicide. For others, you'll have to know the warning signs, which fall into two categories: what the student says and what the student does.

+ What the Student Says

Teenagers experiencing this kind of emotional pain may communicate it verbally, although perhaps in a disguised way. The types of verbal warnings may include any of the following:

• Any comment that implies life isn't worth the effort. For instance, "Life's too painful; I don't think I want to deal with it anymore."

• Any comment that shows the youth believes there's no solution to his or her problems. For example, "There's no way out of this mess."

• Any statement implying that others would be "better off" if the person wasn't around.

• An offer to give up some essential possessions because the student will no longer need them. For example, "You can have my letter jacket; I don't think I'll need it."

• Any indication that the student may take revenge by hurting him or herself. For instance, "She'll wish she hadn't said that when I'm gone."

+ What the Student Does

Sometimes a suicide attempt is impulsive, but sometimes it isn't, and the person begins to plan for it. The student may begin to give away personal items, plan a suicide note, or engage in dangerous activities such as increasing alcohol and drug use. Other signs include dramatic mood changes, intense anxiety, or signs of depression. Most important, if the person has begun to develop a plan, such as buying a weapon, storing up pills, or thinking of a specific scenario such as jumping off a nearby bridge, he or she is at *high* risk for suicide.

ADDITIONAL RESOURCES

+ Books
The Power to Prevent Suicide: A Guide for Teens Helping Teens. Richard Nelson and Judith Galas. Minneapolis: Free Spirit Publishing, 1994.

When Nothing Matters Anymore: A Survival Guide for Depressed Teens. Bev Cobain. Minneapolis: Free Spirit Publishing, 2004.

+ Online Resources
www.stopasuicide.org (Screening for Mental Health, Inc.)

www.suicidepreventionlifeline.org
(National Suicide Prevention Lifeline)

www.suicidology.org (American Association of Suicidology)

SCRIPTURE HELP

+ **Psalms 25:4-7, 15-21**
+ **Isaiah 40:10**
+ **Matthew 10:29-31**
+ **Matthew 11:28-30**
+ **John 3:16**
+ **Romans 8:35-39**
+ **2 Corinthians 1:3-11**
+ **2 Corinthians 12:7-10**
+ **Philippians 1:19-26**
+ **1 Peter 5:7-10**

Care Tips

When there is an immediate threat of suicide, the first step is to ensure the student gets the help needed to be safe.

+ Stay calm.
Take a deep breath and say a silent prayer for protection and comfort for the student.

+ Ask the student directly, "Are you thinking about committing suicide?"
Many people hesitate to ask this question because they're concerned that it will offend the person or will plant the idea in his or her mind. This is a myth. You're more likely to communicate genuine concern and that you understand the seriousness of the situation. This question will also help you determine if the student has a specific plan.

+ Take the problem seriously and express your concern.
Never doubt that the student is actually considering suicide. Instead, assure him or her that you will be supportive in this crisis. Listen carefully without judgment or criticism.

+ Get help immediately.
If your student is willing to get help, take him or her to the local emergency room or mental health center. If your student is not willing to get help, call the National Suicide Prevention Lifeline or 911 (see the "When to Refer" box on page 33).

Counseling Tips

By now, you have helped your student engage in professional help. Now your job is to support the professional services your student is receiving. Your contributions may include any of the following:

+ Openly communicate about suicidal feelings.
Your student will need to talk about these feelings with someone besides a counselor. Don't be afraid to ask if he or she is continuing to have suicidal thoughts. You won't be planting these thoughts if they aren't already there.

+ Follow up.
Agree to meet with the student individually or with the family. You can ask open-ended questions about how the student is doing in different aspects of his or her life, as well as how the therapy is going. Family members will need ongoing support as the student progresses. Check in with family members to see how they are coping.

+ Involve the student in activities.
Do what you can to integrate the student as soon as possible into the scheduled activities of your ministry again. This will help decrease the student's isolation and give him or her some pro-social activities to look forward to.

Group Tips

+ Create a welcoming atmosphere in your ministry.

Make sure all students feel welcomed into your program and youth community. Train your leaders and volunteers in practical welcoming tactics. Try creating a S.A.L.T. atmosphere by training your leaders and students to introduce themselves by asking:

> **S:** Where to do you go to *school*?
>
> **A:** What *activities* are you involved in?
>
> **L:** What do you do in your *leisure* time (or for fun)?
>
> **T:** *Take* your new friend and introduce him or her to some one else who starts the process all over again.

+ Never promise to keep secrets.

Be upfront with your students about confidentiality. Instead of promising that you will keep a secret for a student, remind the student that you'll focus on his or her best interest at all times. You really do care, and although you may not always understand what the student is facing, you will find those who do and will stand by the student through the process of finding answers.

+ Build relationships, not a program.

Sometimes we get so busy building the elements of our programs that we squeeze out the time to build relationships. As youth workers we need to worry less about our lessons and more about the relationships we build with students. These relationships will help your students feel connected, which removes the isolation that leads to suicidal behavior.

+ Pray together.

In the student's emotional state, he or she may have difficulty perceiving God as loving and benevolent. You may need to model God's love for your student until he or she is able to connect with God again. Group prayer is an important and supportive way of manifesting God's love to your teenagers.

WHEN A GROUP MEMBER COMMITS SUICIDE

Sometimes, despite everyone's prayers, support, and love, the worst happens: Someone in your group commits suicide. How you respond to the tragedy is critical for your group.

+ Don't let guilt destroy you.

You may question everything you said, you may doubt everything you did, you may feel that you should have done more. Don't blame yourself for the person's death. Don't let guilt stop you from supporting the other teenagers and leaders in your group. Do seek a professional counselor if you feel that would help you in the grieving process.

+ Grieve with your group.

Your group members and leaders will probably go through the stages of grief (see Chapter 1, "Grief"). Each member will travel through the stages at a different pace and in a different order. Don't be afraid to express your own feelings to the group; this may model a healthy way of grieving to others.

+ Be aware of how you discuss the event.

Avoid sensationalistic, detailed descriptions of the means of suicide; don't give a simplistic picture of why the person may have committed this act ("because his girlfriend broke up with him"); and don't discuss the person or event in ways that could glorify the person or the suicidal act. Do present clear facts and encourage discussion about students' feelings.

What Not to Say

+ "I dare you to do it."

Don't laugh—this happens, and people who say it are usually well-intentioned. People think that they'll call the person's bluff by essentially telling him or her to do it. This is a *bad* idea. In the person's hopeless state of mind, it may be further evidence that he or she isn't valued.

+ "Sure, I promise not to tell anyone."

Don't let a teenager swear you to secrecy. Also, don't worry if you have already agreed to secrecy. Let your student know why you won't be able to keep the agreement—he or she may initially be upset, but will thank you in the long run. Feel confident that it's in your teenager's best interest to speak with others.

+ "Suicide is a sin."

The last thing the hurting student needs is an intellectual or theological debate. Instead, he or she is probably craving someone who can be there emotionally. You can be far more helpful if you work hard to empathize with your student and convince him or her to seek professional help.

What to Say

+ "Let *us* be hopeful for you until you're ready to be hopeful again."

This implies several important things. First, it communicates that every-one is going to be there to support the student. Second, it says that you understand how hopeless your student feels right now. Third, it communicates that you're confident your teenager will emerge from this and be hopeful again.

+ "I know this is an issue that people don't talk enough about in the church. When you feel ready, would you be willing to work with me to start a support group for people feeling depressed and suicidal?"

It's very important to communicate that the student is not alone. By saying this, you imply that others in your ministry share the student's struggles and feelings, and that people need to be supportively discussing the topic more often in the church. And the idea that the student could contribute to helping others is likely to increase his or her sense of self-worth.

+ "What can I do to help?"

This question communicates that you genuinely care for the student and love him or her in Christ. Your student may be feeling as if no one cares or no one cares enough to reach out. This will dispel that false belief. You also don't impose your own ideas about what would be helpful, but you allow the student's unique needs to guide you. An important thing to remember: If you make this offer, be sure you're ready to back it up, regardless of the time and effort required!

CHAPTER FOUR

Addictions
Offering Love and Support to Those Who Are Trying to Quit

with counseling insights from **KELLY M. FLANAGAN, PH.D**
+ ministry tips from **SUMMER RIVERS SALOMONSEN**

The following story represents the experience of two friends: one, falling deeper and deeper into alcohol and drug addiction, and the other, trying desperately to bring her back.

She got the call at 2 a.m. "Emily. I'm on my way." Starting up the car in the cold of the early morning, Susan began to pray. "God, I need you here. Give me your wisdom. Touch her heart." She slowed at the beginning of the street and gazed down the long stretch of houses. The party street. Notorious for all-nighters, endless beer, and assorted drugs. "God, I need your guidance."

Pulling to the curb in front of the house, she rolled down the window and peered through what seemed an endless group of people. Where was she? Getting out of the car, she walked toward the front of the house, scanning the crowd, and saw her sitting on a side porch, with her head in her hands. "Hey, Em." Emily didn't look up. Her hair was smeared with vomit, and she reeked of smoke. "Let's get you home."

Susan drove home, silently. Emily rested her head against the cracked window and moaned. So many thoughts, so many things she wanted to share, but she remained silent, praying. "Sorry," Emily faintly whispered.

Susan glanced over, touching her hand in response. "I love you. You're going to be OK."

She made up the futon and pulled the blanket over Emily, who had already passed out. Susan wondered what would become of her friend. It hadn't always been like this. Emily used to be different, but over the years she had chosen things that Susan wouldn't. Regardless, their friendship had never faltered, and Susan still believed that somewhere inside, Emily knew that God desired more for her than this.

Early Saturday morning, Susan sat by Emily's bed, staring at her friend. Emily awoke bleary and confused. She sat up and gathered her thoughts for a long time. "I missed small group," she said, matter-of-factly.

"Yes. We all missed you."

"Thank you for getting me."

"I will always come for you, because I love you and because that is what God asks me to do."

Emily looked away, wiped her eyes, and put on her clothes. "I have to get home—I told Mom I'd be spending the night here, but I have to be home by 9 a.m. We're going shopping." And with that, Emily left.

Several days passed before they spoke again, and yet Susan committed her friend to prayer. With the help of her youth group, Susan was able to share her frustrations, feelings, and hopes for Emily's recovery. This situation was not improving, and it was getting harder and harder to remember the old Emily, the one she knew before the addiction took hold. However, Susan knew that God was working, and she knew that she would remain committed to Emily, no matter what.

On faith, Susan asked Emily if she would come to the youth group's planned winter retreat in the mountains. "It will be fun!" was her only ploy. "It will be a good time to relax and be together. What do you think?"

Emily looked away. "I don't feel like I'm part of that group anymore."

Susan hesitated. "Maybe not, but you're my friend, and I'm inviting you. Please come."

Emily shrugged and nodded. "But I'm only riding with you."

"Fine, we'll make plans later."

It was Friday afternoon and Susan began packing her suitcase for the weekend retreat. She laid it out on the bed, glanced at the clock, and placed two outfits inside. Rummaging through her closet for her winter boots, she glanced at the clock again, paused, and grabbed the phone. She reached Emily's voice mail. "Em, it's me. Just checking in. I'm almost done packing and wanted to swing by around 5. Let's grab something to eat on the way up. The others are meeting us there...give me a call."

As it neared 4 o'clock, Susan still hadn't heard back. She began to pace the room. Pausing, she fell to her knees and asked for God's help. Then, she called her youth group leader and asked for prayer. "Something's not right. Please pray."

At 5 o'clock the phone rang. "Susan?" It was Emily, but she sounded different.

"Where are you? Are you OK?" Silence. Susan heard something like dripping water in the background. "Emily, talk to me." She heard the repressed sob, more silence. Susan waited.

"I used again."

The moment had come—the moment that always came, even after Emily seemed like she was going to quit for good this time. Susan had been hearing this for years; she had watched her friend fall from the light and time after time seek out an addiction that took her farther and farther away from God.

"I don't know who I am anymore. I feel so far away from God. I can't find my way back."

Susan remained silent. This was the moment she had prayed for and hoped for—Emily had never talked about God's role in relation to the addiction before. She let the Holy Spirit minister to her friend in her darkest hour. For six full minutes, the two friends sat in silence: one in a bathtub and the other leaned over her kitchen table. Susan could hear Emily standing up. She could only pray that Jesus had spoken to Emily there in the tub. Susan continued to pray as she waited for Emily to speak. Hearing the water swell on the other line, hearing the towel taken off the rack, hearing the muffled sound of cloth to phone, still she prayed.

Finally, Emily spoke. "I'm so sorry, Jesus. I'm so sorry."

Still holding the phone to her ear, Susan loaded her suitcase in her car and drove over to Emily's house where she was waiting on the steps. Ending the call, Susan silently loaded up her friend's bag, opened her door, and hugged her. The two embraced for a long time, crying. Finally, Emily pulled away, and Susan was amazed to see the light in her eyes. She knew that this wouldn't be the end of her friend's struggles, but she also knew that Emily was seeking the light, and God would reveal himself to her.

As true friends, they drove up the mountainside together, eating hamburgers, content in silence. As they reached the campground, Emily looked over, leaning her head against the seat, and said, "Thank you."

SCRIPTURE HELP

+ **Psalm 26:2-3**
+ **Psalm 37:5**
+ **Psalm 139:23-24**
+ **Proverbs 16:3**
+ **Proverbs 20:1**
+ **Ephesians 5:15-18**
+ **Philippians 4:13**
+ **Colossians 3:1-2**
+ **Titus 2:6-7**
+ **I Peter 4:1-4**

Care and Counseling Tips

THE BASICS

Addiction is a term with broad and sometimes uncertain definitions. In general, an addiction may be present when an individual is dependent on something and cannot resist the temptation to partake in it: alcohol, illicit drugs, painkillers, prescription drugs, pornography, gambling, computer gaming, food, shopping, or even high-risk behavior such as shoplifting. How do you know if someone is dependent on something? The following criteria may serve as signs that an addiction is present:

+ Tolerance.
"I can drink an entire six-pack right now and not even feel the effects."

+ Withdrawal.
Psychological: "I just can't stop thinking about pornography."
Physical: "I can't stop shaking; I really need a drink."

+ Engaging in more of the problematic behavior than intended.
"I only meant to buy one thing, but ended up spending a thousand dollars."

+ Routine, unsuccessful attempts to quit the behavior.
"I quit smoking three times this month. And each time it only lasted a day."

+ Problems in daily functioning at work, home, or social settings.
"I couldn't go to class twice last week because I got high before school started."

+ An inability to stop despite awareness of negative consequences.

"My parents will kick me out if I keep this up, but I still can't help myself."

WHEN TO REFER

+ **The addiction has become physically dangerous.**
+ **The addiction significantly impairs relationships.**
+ **You observe withdrawal symptoms or the student acknowledges them.**
+ **The student begins to experience depression or anxiety after stopping the addictive behavior.**

Care Tips

Try these steps to support your student who is struggling with an addiction:

✛ Assess the student's level of desire to change.

Your course of action will differ depending on where the student is on the "stages of change" scale:

• *Precontemplation*: At this stage, the person is unaware of the problem and resistant to change. The most effective approach at this stage is to communicate acceptance of the student and lack of judgment. Allow him or her to develop trust in you and your opinions so that when you eventually share your perspective, the teenager will be less defensive.

• *Contemplation*: Now the student recognizes the presence of a problem, but is probably more interested in learning about it than doing anything to change it. Your best approach at this stage is to gently increase his or her motivation for change. Your actions will be most helpful and accepted if characterized by empathy, support, and a genuine attitude of concern.

• *Preparation*: At this stage, the person will express, for the first time, a determination to change the behavior. However, he or she may still not have a clear sense of how to change. You can continue to provide support and help the student implement a plan of action.

✛ Gather information.

Examine the teenager's life for problems that may drive a need to flee from reality. Assess the level of use of the substance or behavior. Determine which behaviors came first, and under what circumstances. The more information you gather, the better you can appreciate the student's situation and the more the student will feel understood.

✛ Make a relapse-prevention plan.

After identifying situations that might put your student at risk, help him or her come up with a written plan to avoid them. For example, for a teenager addicted to pornography, encourage the family to relocate their computer to a high-traffic area, or to install monitoring software. A meth-amphetamine addict may need to avoid situations where he or she can easily obtain a large amount of cash so the drug will not be easily accessible. The more built-in accountability, the better.

+ Surround with support.

Help the student form relationships with other teenagers in recovery. Finding 12-step programs in your area is easy; see the "Additional Resources" section in this chapter for Web sites. You can also contact local churches; many meetings take place in churches. Also promote healthy relationships with other students in your group who don't share the addiction. These connections can help students spend their time on more productive activities.

Counseling Tips

Recovery from any kind of addiction can be a long road. Take these steps to develop a realistic view of supporting a student with an addiction:

+ Educate yourself.
It's a good idea to know which drugs or behaviors are popular in your area. They can change from time to time, based on the availability of particular substances or the introduction of new activities to the area. You should stay on top of what young people are exposed to. The students themselves can be a great source of such information, or meet regularly with others who work with teenagers, like other youth pastors or school staff in your area.

+ Understand denial.
If you recognize a potential addiction problem, but the student doesn't, use confrontation gently and respectfully. Point out inconsistencies or realities that the student would rather not face. Don't argue; the best approach is persistence rather than power.

+ Understand relapse.
Many addiction treatment professionals agree that relapse is an expected part of recovery. The temptation to relapse doesn't represent failure. Help your student deal with the painful realization that the temptation will always be present. Offer ongoing accountability as a symbol of your long-term dedication to his or her recovery.

Group Tips

Witnessing the damaging effects of addiction can leave every believer feeling helpless and without options. But acting alone is never what God has in mind. As a group, God has blessed Christians with the unifying power of faith and hope that only comes through his love. As you reach out to a struggling individual, remember to make use of each other through fellowship.

+ Stand guard.
A person buried by addiction will have a long road to recovery once he or she sees the light. Be prepared to make yourselves available to this person at all hours. Sign up for different "posts" that include both night and day. Though the experience will be harrowing, God will bless your commitment.

+ Pray. Pray. Pray.
If you've heard it once, you've heard it a hundred times: Christians are called upon to pray in times of trial! Make use of this unique power by establishing a prayer chain for your group. Remember: Pray without ceasing!

+ Welcome back to the world.
Those who struggle with addictions have spent a long time in darkness and will have a difficult time adjusting to a life that doesn't include the addiction. Within your group, commit to spending active time with this person, enjoying fun activities such as going to the movies, cooking dinner, exercising, or volunteering.

+ Promote healthy living.
Addictions rob a person of the balance that God intended, both physically and spiritually. Encouraging a healthy lifestyle during the transition back

into living will go a long way toward promoting a long-term change. Plan group dinners and activities like bowling and ice-skating.

+ Be ready for a fall.

Beating addiction is never easy and usually requires a few setbacks before the person is free. A simple note or phone call will remind this person how valuable they are to the group, and will most likely help to alleviate the power of addiction as it rears its head during recovery.

What Not to Say

+ "Addiction is a spiritual disease; you must not be right with God."

Although many people who recover from addiction do find that spiritual growth is a key part of the process, it's not fair to tell a student that addiction is *only* a spiritual disease. The hurting student may be working hard on his or her spiritual life, but other biological and emotional factors may be interfering.

+ "Just stop."

Saying this shows a misunderstanding of the nature of addiction. Whether it be drugs, alcohol, or gaming, addiction is powerful and beating it is no small feat.

+ "You really shouldn't be doing drugs."

Most likely, a student even loosely involved with the church will recognize that the addiction is wrong. Saying this will alienate the student and will ultimately defeat your purpose of helping the student overcome the addiction.

What to Say

+ "I care about you."

Use language that is direct and personal. The student will remember your compassion, even if not acknowledging it.

+ "We are praying for you."

Say this and mean it. Making use of the power of prayer over addiction is the smartest move you can make. Letting your student know you're praying will open your student's eyes to how valuable he or she is.

+ "This situation is not too big for God."

Addiction can feel overwhelming and suffocating. Those who struggle with it will certainly doubt whether or not God's power is strong enough. Reassure them with compassion, not with judgment.

ADDITIONAL RESOURCES

+ Books

Alcoholics Anonymous. Big Book, Fourth Edition. Alcoholics Anonymous World Services, Inc., 2001. (You can also find the big book online at the AA Web site listed below.)

Drugs, Society, and Human Behavior. Ninth Edition. Oakley Ray and Charles Ksir. New York: McGraw-Hill Higher Education, 2001.

+ Online Resources

www.alcoholics-anonymous.org (Alcoholics Anonymous)

www.na.org (Narcotics Anonymous)

www.xxxchurch.com
(Christian support for people addicted to pornography)

FINDING A 12-STEP GROUP

To find a local 12-step group, check with local churches (many meetings take place in churches). Or write General Service Office, Box 459, Grand Central Station, New York, NY, 10163, for a list of AA-approved groups.

The 12 Steps of Alcoholics Anonymous:

1. We admitted we were powerless over alcohol—that our lives had become unmanageable.

2. Came to believe that a Power greater than ourselves could restore us to sanity.

3. Made a decision to turn our will and our lives over to the care of God *as we understood Him.*

4. Made a searching and fearless moral inventory of ourselves.

5. Admitted to God, to ourselves, and to another human being the exact nature of our wrongs.

6. Were entirely ready to have God remove all these defects of character.

7. Humbly asked Him to remove our shortcomings.

8. Made a list of all persons we had harmed and became willing to make amends to them all.

9. Made direct amends to such people wherever possible, except when to do so would injure them or others.

10. Continued to take personal inventory and when we were wrong promptly admitted it.

11. Sought through prayer and meditation to improve our conscious contact with God, *as we understood Him*, praying only for knowledge of His will for us and the power to carry that out.

12. Having had a spiritual awakening as the result of these steps, we tried to carry this message to alcoholics and to practice these principles in all our affairs.

CHAPTER FIVE

Divorce
Supporting Your Student Through Family Changes

with counseling insights from **TERRI S. WATSON, PSY.D.**
+ ministry tips from **BRIAN DIEDE**

What really happened was that my dad left. He and my mom had been fighting, but I didn't realize it had gotten so bad. When I would come home from school, usually just one of my parents was home. If they were both home at the same time, my two brothers and I had to walk on eggshells around them. It seemed like one little thing could just set them off, and mostly they would blame each other for things we did wrong.

What I remember is that I'd had a bad dream, woke up, and heard my parents fighting. I don't think they were fighting specifically about me, but I felt like their yelling was my fault. It was the following morning that I woke up to find my dad had gone and my mom was still there—but she was now just a shell who went through the motions of taking care of me and my brothers.

My dad's job took him away from home at times, so for him to be gone for a day or two wasn't that out of the ordinary. One day I noticed it had been weeks since I'd seen my dad. Strangely, the next time I saw him, he showed up at our house with a police officer. He went in the house without saying much. He grabbed a few things, gave me a hug, and said he would not see me for a while, but he loved me very much.

The next day, my mom, my two brothers, and I were driving in the car and I vividly remember the way she explained to us that mommy and daddy had decided they would not be living together anymore, but he would still be our dad and we would still get to see him—just not as often as we used to.

My mom got custody of my brothers and me, and we only saw Dad every other weekend. Trying to adjust to this new way of living was difficult, to say the least. Leaving Mom on the weekends, and then leaving Dad to go back, brought about huge emotional crashes that only got more complicated when Dad's new life took him to the other side of the country. Now my brothers and I fly to see him every summer for two weeks. I really miss my friends when we are there.

In some ways, things are better. My parents are pretty good about not fighting in front of us anymore, and they try to be civil with each other when they need to arrange something for us. It still feels like I have to walk on eggshells, though, especially if my mom asks something about my dad or his girlfriend. It feels like I'm going back and forth between two warring planets—each with its own set of rules, customs, and even language. And I don't really fit in either place.

To say that the divorce has been hard would not be sufficient. There have been numerous occasions—both past and present—where the effects of the divorce have presented themselves. I've been feeling more depressed recently, and sometimes I feel like the divorce was my fault. Also, I like living with my mom and of course I love her, but sometimes I miss having my dad around for guy time.

Right after the divorce, when I was younger, I had to draw a picture of my family in school. I was confused about who to include. My mom and my brothers? That's who I lived with. My dad and his new girlfriend? I didn't see him much anymore since he moved to another state. I ended up drawing everyone in separate carts on a Ferris wheel, with confusing lines connecting us. That's still how I feel—like I'm looming over empty space, all alone in my cart. We're all still connected, but it's hard to figure out how.

My mom treats my oldest brother like he's her best friend. He had to take on a lot more responsibility when my dad left: watching my brother and me, cleaning up around the house, listening to my mom talk about her loneliness. She has really relied on him—but sometimes he seems confused about his role in our family. Is he the son or the parent? He's always telling me what to do, and he never gets any time to just be a teenager with his friends.

I guess I deal with it by watching my older brothers deal with it. If they get sad or happy or mad about anything…that's what I do. I am the youngest of three, and that's how you learn. I also have a few friends whose parents are divorced, so they understand what it's like. I know my parents still love me, and I still, today, love them both with all my heart. They are my two favorite people on the planet.

Care and Counseling Tips

THE BASICS

Families and teenagers face numerous challenges during a divorce: the initial transition from a two-parent household, the adjustment to two households, and later, remarriage. While there are important cultural and religious differences in the meaning and experience of divorce, most teenagers and families experience common challenges:

+ Initial Impact

This stage is a transition involving feelings of grief, confusion, anxiety, and loss of confidence. Teenagers may feel responsible for the breakup or feel they failed to prevent it. They also face changes including relocation, adjustment to two households, and a change in standard of living.

+ Single Parenthood

Teenagers in this stage may experience increased responsibility for younger siblings, loss of financial resources, and the need to reevaluate relationships with their parents. They may become their parent's "best friend" instead of having a parent-child relationship.

+ Blended Families

This stage involves allowing new family members into a teenager's life, including stepparents, stepsiblings, and others. The student may struggle with divided loyalties between two parents. There may also be a conflict between maintaining social relationships and maintaining parental visitation rights.

Care Tips

During the initial crisis of a divorce or separation, use these tips with your teenagers:

+ Facilitate communication between parents and students.

Help parents talk to teenagers about divorce in an age-appropriate way—for example, reassuring them that the divorce is not their fault, explaining why the parents are divorcing, and conveying what will happen next. It may help the family for you to be present as a neutral third party during these discussions.

+ Encourage parents to keep their separation low-conflict.

Remind the parents to be cooperative despite their personal differences. Help them come up with ways to enhance communication between them. For example, parents could pass a notebook back and forth between visits to keep each other informed about medical needs, school assignments, or upcoming events. As much as possible, help parents negotiate conflicts without placing the teenager in the middle.

+ Create a neutral setting.

When counseling divorcing families, establish the church as a safe place for healing and support. Avoid making judgments, taking sides, and placing blame. Focus on creating solutions for the future, not on rehashing the past.

+ Help your teenager set boundaries.

Often your student will need to take on more responsibilities at home, but this should not interfere with normal developmental needs. A teenager may also need help in discouraging parents from sharing too much personal information with him or her or putting down the other parent.

Counseling Tips

As families move on and readjust after a divorce, stay involved by using these suggestions:

+ Provide resources.

As parents reestablish themselves separately, they may find that the new challenges of daily living require additional resources. Provide referrals for child care, shelter, food, financial assistance, or vocational training. Help single parents establish a support network, including extended family, church fellowship, and other single parents.

+ Help parents establish authority.

Support single parents in the presence of the teenager, encouraging the teenager to respect and obey the parent. In blended families, counsel the biological parent to maintain the primary responsibility for disciplining the teenager. This will give the new spouse time to develop a relationship with the teenager before trying to move into the role of a parent.

+ Be there to listen.

Keep open communication with the teenager as the family continues to change. Many teenagers have conflicting feelings about the divorce, the idea of parents dating or remarrying, and visitation schedules. Students may feel caught in the middle of the two homes. Establish a trusting relationship with your student so he or she will have a safe place to talk about these issues as they arise.

+ Find model marriages.

Children of divorce experience anxiety and self-doubt about their ability to establish successful love relationships. Help your teenager identify couples with successful marriages in your church or ministry to model relationships after. Encourage your student to realize that he or she can make independent choices. Remind the student that every couple experiences problems and that no marriage is perfect, but a successful marriage is possible for him or her in the future.

SCRIPTURE HELP

+ **Psalm 27:1-6**
+ **Psalm 51:10-12**
+ **Psalm 121**
+ **Ecclesiastes 3:1-11**
+ **Isaiah 43:2-3**

+ **Jeremiah 29:11**
+ **Romans 8:26**
+ **2 Corinthians 1:3-5**
+ **2 Corinthians 4:7-8**
+ **Philippians 2:12-13**

ADDITIONAL RESOURCES

+ Books

Blended Families: Creating Harmony as You Build a New Home Life. Maxine Marsolini. Chicago: Moody Press, 2000.

The Blended Family: Achieving Peace and Harmony in the Christian Home. Edward Douglas and Sharon Douglas. Franklin, TN: Providence House Publishers, 2000.

Ministering to Twenty-First Century Families: Eight Big Ideas for Church Leaders. Dennis Rainey. Nashville, TN: W Publishing Group, 2001.

+ Online Resources

www.parentswithoutpartners.org (Parents Without Partners)

www.stepfamilies.info (National Stepfamily Resource Center)

Group Tips

+ Continue to welcome the student.

People work through difficult situations differently. Some students will want to have people around them, and they'll want to talk about the situation. Be a listening ear for them. Other students will want to be alone. Give those students space and time to think, but keep a close eye on them. If you notice a student becoming isolated, invite him or her to an outing where there will be a small group of people. In either case, encourage the other students in your group to be welcoming and understanding to the student during this difficult time.

+ Provide a place to belong.

Offering a place of true belonging goes a long way in combating the feelings of isolation that are a part of divorce. Be explicit in your commitment as a group to walk through this difficult experience with the student.

+ Ask.

Don't be afraid to ask the student how he or she is handling the parents' divorce. You may have to ask about that subject specifically—if you simply ask how things are going in a general way, your student might skirt around the issue and not tell you about what's truly going on.

+ Make a connection.

It's important for your student to know that he or she is not alone in this experience. If there are some older teenagers, college students, young adults, or adults in your church who have been through a divorce of their parents, set up a meeting time for them to get together and talk. Invite a special speaker to come to your youth events to share testimonies, or have someone who has gone through the experience of parents divorcing share a testimony about that time in his or her life.

+ Pray.

Don't just say that you are going to pray for your student—actually pray. Don't be afraid to ask the student if you can pray for him or her after you have just got done talking about the divorce. Continue to pray for the student throughout the day.

WHEN TO REFER

Provide a referral to a mental health professional if you notice any of the following:

+ **The student's responses to family changes begin to interfere with school, social relationships, or behavior.**
+ **Ongoing, damaging conflict is occurring between parents.**
+ **The student begins to isolate or references self-destructive or suicidal thoughts or feelings.**

What Not to Say

+ "The Bible says that God hates divorce."

Although the Bible does clearly say that, this is not something to say to someone whose parents are going through a divorce. Since the divorce is not the student's fault, he or she needs to feel supported, not criticized.

+ "That same thing happened to one of my friends. It's no big deal."

Downplaying the situation doesn't help your student with his or her questions, feelings, and hurt. Your student needs to know that your care for him or her is unique and personal.

+ "Whose fault do you think it is?"

It's easy to blame people in a divorce situation. The parents might be talking bad about the other spouse, and your student might be feeling stuck in the middle of the fight. Even worse, the student might be blaming him or herself. There isn't one single event or person that caused this divorce. Help the student see that the reason for this divorce is very complex.

What to Say

+ "I don't know what to say."

If you don't know what to say, don't avoid speaking to the student! Just approach him or her and try this statement—and be open for whatever conversation comes up.

+ "Sorry to hear about this."

Hearing this sincere comment can help the student know that you care and that you won't judge or lecture. The student may want helpful advice later on, but your first reaction should be one of sorrow, sadness, and empathy.

+ "What are your thoughts and feelings about this divorce?"

It's important for the student to have someone to talk with. Your student may want to share all the thoughts and emotions he or she has surrounding the divorce. Anger, hurt, and confusion are natural reactions. It's important to let the student express those emotions.

+ "How do you think your life will change now that your parents are getting divorced?"

Many changes are coming up for the student. Will the student live with Mom or Dad? Will he or she have to move to a different city or state? Will your student have to make new friends? Will Mom and Dad still love them?

Change is difficult and it can cause the student to be stressed out. It's important for your student to know that he or she can talk about these changes with you.

A "HEALTHY" DIVORCE

Although a divorce is rarely a welcome or positive experience in a person's life, a "healthy" divorce is possible—one that minimizes the damage to all individuals involved. If possible, help the parents of your youth strive for these goals:

+ **Both parents remain involved with the children in order to provide a continued sense of "family."**

+ **Both parents are protecting the children and teenagers from the negative aspects of the divorce.**

+ **Both spouses are able to accept and integrate the divorce into their thinking about themselves and their future in a healthy way.**

CHAPTER SIX

Abuse
Empowering Victims to
Regain Control of Their Lives

with counseling insights from
SCOTT GIBSON, M.S.W., L.C.S.W.
+ ministry tips from JEREMY HOLBURN

Like many teenagers, 16-year-old Kaylee was the victim of physical, emotional, and sexual abuse. This is her story.

Emergency Response Handbook: *Please tell us about your background and experience with abuse.*

Kaylee: There was a lot of abuse in my house when I was a kid, and some of the most damaging wasn't the most obvious. My mom was both physically and emotionally abusive; she would "spank" my sister and me on a daily basis, which consisted of her punching us in a blind rage. Afterward, she would sob and hold us and tell us she did it for our good—that she was a good mother. Some days she would leave and not come home. Sometimes she would leave angry, threatening to kill herself, and other times she would just go without a word. When she would come home, she would act as if nothing was wrong. After one of these absences, my sister, who was 17 at the time, left home for good. All of my mother's anger was then directed toward me.

When I was 5, my mother started prostituting me out to various men. They paid to have sex with me. My mother told me this needed to happen because we were getting less money from the state and we all needed to contribute as much as we could. Most of the men who paid were men from the church we attended. I remember going to church on Sundays and listening to one of the men: He would preach about God's love and holiness to a congregation littered with other men who had raped me. It was awful, but I didn't know I was worth more than that.

Years later, when I was put in foster care and all of this came out, my therapist and caseworker went back to my elementary school and asked if they had suspected abuse. The teachers all said they did, but didn't do anything to help me because they weren't sure.

In middle school, I started acting out, getting suspended from school for fighting. My mom and I would get into fistfights, and eventually, the cops would come. The state and courts became involved, and eventually also Family Preservation Services. The authorities took me away shortly thereafter and put me in foster care for parental-child conflict. For three years I was in custody, and nobody asked me why I was so angry—and I never mentioned my abuse.

ERH: *What impact did this abuse have on you, and how did you deal with it?*

Kaylee: I experienced many other physical, sexual, and emotional assaults through my adolescence, but I felt too used up to care. I felt ruined, and nothing seemed significant because nobody had made a big deal about it before. I was always sullen and angry, crazy with rage and filled with all these emotions I didn't know what to do with. I would say the meanest, most hateful things. I was angry, but more than that, I was hurt. My relationships were unstable at best and usually based on getting what I needed. After being in 32 homes in four years and going to six different high schools, I graduated from high school.

ERH: *With whom in your youth group did you share about your abuse? Tell about these conversations.*

Kaylee: I went to church the whole time I was in foster care. I mentioned once to the youth pastor's wife, Lynn, that I had been raped. I remember her holding me and telling me it was OK to cry, even though I didn't. I was mainly worried she would tell someone, and begged her not to. She promised she wouldn't.

Later, I attended another church with my friend, and the youth group became one of my favorite activities. Soon after becoming involved, I wrote a letter to my youth pastor, Mike, hinting that I may have been sexually abused. He called me to his office and told me I needed to be very careful with what I told him because he was bound by law to report it. He said it could ruin my life and a lot of other people's lives, too. I decided not to share about the abuse with anybody else.

ERH: *What are you glad the youth group did for you? What do you wish the group would have done differently?*

Kaylee: The youth group in Lynn's church was wonderful. Lynn and her husband never treated me differently because of my past; they would challenge me and call me out on inappropriate behavior. They held me to the same standards they held everyone else to, and that gave me a sense of normalcy.

In the other cases, I wish the youth pastors would have taken the time to really get to know me and understand my heart. I wish Mike would have never given me the option not to disclose my abuse. This made me feel like it was something I had control over—like it was my fault. And the way he blew off my hurt and avoided me really impacted my belief system and self-esteem. I wish he would have encouraged me to tell.

ERH: *What's the "end" of your story? How are you doing now, and what's the lasting impact on your life?*

Kaylee: I have a hard time feeling connected, or "bonded," with God. Also, I have a very hard time attending church. However, all in all, I think I am pretty well adjusted. Becoming a Christian has been key in that process. I had to honestly look at who God is…not who people had taught me God is, not what I could conclude based on past events…but honestly look at what the Bible says. To see God's true nature for myself, for the very first time, and make a choice based on facts was a healing thing.

Of course, my past has had an impact on my relationships, but that isn't the person who I am today. I am happy, I have a lot of friends, and I don't curse at people or fly off the handle because I honestly have nothing to be angry about. That shift in attitude came with my understanding of who God is. I am blessed that I have gone through so many changes, so I can make a clear distinction between who I was compared to who I am now. It helps me keep my past in the past.

Care and Counseling Tips

THE BASICS

When children are abused at a young age, it is common for the emotional damage of the abuse to surface in adolescence. There are probably also some teenagers in your ministry who are currently being abused. Some of the abuse may even be from family members who attend your church. Physical, emotional, and sexual abuse sometimes feel like normal family interactions to teenagers who've lived in this environment for most of their lives.

Teenagers also feel the stigma of living in a dysfunctional family. They may be ashamed to invite friends over to their homes or feel pressured to hide the interactions and present the family as being normal. Victims of sexual abuse may feel that the abuse is their fault.

Your ministry can be a safe place for teenagers to experience loving and accepting relationships and to develop a positive sense of self-worth.

Care Tips

Counseling a student who has been sexually, verbally, emotionally, or physically abused is complex. Because of the intense nature of the issue, it's essential that you refer the abused student to a qualified counselor. However, you can be a part of the healing process along with the counselor.

+ Your Initial Response
You may be the first one to hear about the abuse. It's important that you take seriously what the student is saying and commend the student for being brave and telling you about it. Survivors of abuse often keep secrets in order to get through it all. Telling an adult takes a tremendous amount of courage.

+ "It's Not Your Fault"
One of the most important things you can do is to assure the student that the abuse is not his or her fault. This idea can be challenging for abused teenagers to accept. You will probably need to continue reminding your student of this as he or she continues healing.

+ Reporting
The law requires counselors (and in most states, the clergy as well) to report abuse. As a youth worker, it's in the best interest of the student for you to *immediately* act on and report any suspicion of abuse. Be familiar with your church's reporting policies. A good rule of thumb to remember is this: It's not your job to investigate it, but it is your job to report it.

Counseling Tips

Be alert to these specific types of abuse:

+ Sexual Abuse

More than other types of abuse, sexual abuse carries a stigma of shame and humiliation. When children or adolescents are victimized sexually, the sexual feelings they felt, some of which may have been pleasurable, may cause them to feel guilty and confused. When the abuser is a parent, relative, or other person who the child trusts, this pattern of secrecy has usually occurred for a long time. By the time the abuse is reported, the child or adolescent may feel an alliance or loyalty to the abuser. Historically, the church has been a place where sexuality is feared and shamed; students who are being sexually abused may sense this and feel afraid to reveal their struggle.

Create a safe environment in your ministry for students to open up about their experiences. Teenagers will sense they can trust you if you are willing to walk through the healing process with them.

+ Date Rape

Sexual abuse can also occur among students in the same age group, either in the dating environment or in another social setting. Depending on the circumstances, young women (and even young men) can become confused about whether they were abused or whether they "asked for it."

Date rapes often occur in environments with drugs or alcohol. Teach your students to place themselves in safe situations—however, if one of your students is raped in such a situation, be intentional about reminding the student that it's not his or her fault. Remind your students that if they do not want to be sexually intimate yet someone is making them be intimate, that's sexual abuse. You may need to support the student in reporting the date rape to the proper authorities.

+ Bullying

In your ministry, you may also encounter situations in which teenagers' peers are abusing them. Bullying, harassment, and assaults happen often in school and church settings. Bullying ranges from teasing to serious harassment and physical violence. Bullying can be either verbal or physical.

If you suspect that someone is bullying a student, seek help for him or her as soon as possible. Ask the student to tell you what is going on. If he or she is uncomfortable at first, offer to listen to the situation without the student mentioning any names.

Suggest proactive ways for the bullied student to stand up for him or herself. For example, staying in groups with other students and practicing being assertive can help make a bully victim feel empowered. You will also want to involve school authorities if that's where the bullying is taking place.

ADDITIONAL RESOURCES

+ Books

Caring for Sexually Abused Children: A Handbook for Families and Churches. R. Timothy Kearney. Downers Grove, IL: InterVarsity Press, 2001.

The Mosaic Mind: Empowering the Tormented Selves of Child Abuse Survivors. Regina A. Goulding and Richard C. Schwartz. New York: W. W. Norton & Company, 1995.

+ Online Resources

www.helpguide.org (Helpguide; click on "Abuse & Addictions" and then "Child abuse & neglect")

www.safeyouth.org
(National Youth Violence Prevention Resource Center)

Group Tips

+ Pray.

This is the most significant way you can help and support. Don't just pray for the teenager—pray for the entire family, and especially for those who are doing the abusing. Also, praying together will encourage the youth to pray by him or herself.

+ Make connections often.

Everyone needs to feel connected. A phone call, e-mail, or text message can reinforce the fact that the student isn't going through this alone.

+ Provide escape from an unhealthy environment.

Time away from daily routine will give the student a chance to breathe and perhaps even have some fun. Try to provide an occasional escape while meeting the youth's needs.

+ Be available.

Stay active in the victim's life, no matter how overwhelming or draining it may be. Make sure he or she knows how deeply you care. Continue to be a good listener by asking questions about things that are important to your student. Create a sense of normalcy for the student.

+ Love them as God loves them.

Never make students feel they are less, different, or damaged in any way. Make sure they know the truth about themselves. Build them up, encourage them…focus on them, as whole persons, and not just on their abuse.

What Not to Say

+ **"God was right there with you, right by your side, weeping and feeling your pain."**
This well-intentioned comment feels like a slap on a victim's face: If God was right there with me—and he is all-good and all-powerful—how could he just weep and watch that happen? Avoid any comment that might paint God as a passive observer.

+ **"Everything happens for a reason."**
Unless you know what that specific reason is, don't ever say this. It has the power to make abuse victims feel resentful toward a God who would hurt them for some "higher purpose."

+ **"Just remember, there is always someone out there who has it worse than you do."**
As true as this may be, it doesn't change the fact that the teenager is in pain—real, devastating pain. Comparing situations will only minimize a victim's experience.

What to Say

+ **"It wasn't your fault."**
Even if victims say they know this, a lot of times (deep down) they don't. And even if they do, it never hurts to affirm this truth.

+ **"You are precious, beautiful, and valuable."**
Speak truth to youth about themselves. In many cases, all they've ever heard are lies. Remind the student that God loves him or her.

✛ "Can we pray together?"

Spend time before God, and explore the Bible together. Find comfort and healing in God's Word and through the working of the Holy Spirit.

✛ "I don't know what to say."

Don't just try to fill silences. Admit when you don't have the answers, and be content to simply *be* with the teenager…even in total silence. Youth have a keen perception for sincerity and will recognize your Christ-like love.

SCRIPTURE HELP

- ✛ **2 Samuel 22:2-4**
- ✛ **Psalm 10:17-18**
- ✛ **Psalm 23**
- ✛ **Psalm 55:16-17, 22**
- ✛ **Psalm 62:5-6**
- ✛ **Psalm 91:4**
- ✛ **Psalm 143:7-8**
- ✛ **Isaiah 40:29-31**
- ✛ **2 Corinthians 1:3-7**
- ✛ **1 Peter 5:7**

WHEN TO REFER

Report any suspicions you have of abuse. Some or all of the following symptoms indicate a student is being abused or has been abused:

Poor self-image, unusual interest in or avoidance of things of a sexual nature, sexually acting out, depression, withdrawal, anger, aggressiveness, self-destructive behaviors, anxiety, problems sleeping, fear of new relationships or situations, school problems, flashbacks, nightmares, drug or alcohol abuse, physical signs of maltreatment

CHAPTER SEVEN

Crisis Pregnancy

Loving Students Through Unplanned
Pregnancy or Post-Abortion Stress

with counseling insights from **COLLEEN J. ALDEN, M.A.**

+ ministry tips from **CHRISTINA SCHOFIELD**

I know a real-life Wonder Woman, minus the spandex and red go-go boots.

Lynnie. She's one of my best friends. She's like a big sister to everyone and chock-full of joy. My favorite thing about her is the way she throws her head back and laughs with her mouth wide open—a great laugh coming from all the way down in her toes.

Lynnie is the person you would expect to have the answers about all of life's problems, not by forging through them, but by wisely avoiding them. But then, she will look at you squarely with those dark soulful eyes and set the record straight. Her voice lowers as she explains that her life has not been easy, but it has been blessed.

As a teenager she was headed toward destruction. "I was doing drugs and sleeping around, actually keeping count of the guys I had been with. It was a game of conquering and comfort," she recalls. "The guys I chose I had just danced with or we had shared a drink. It didn't matter."

Then, the game took an unexpected turn. She found out she was pregnant, and she wasn't sure who the father was. "I was getting bigger by the day, and increasingly lonely. I was humbled—my cute shape was gone, my boyfriend was gone, and I was alone on Mother's Day."

Even in the best of circumstances, finding out you are pregnant is freaky. There are changes to your body. There is fear of the unknown. There are sacrifices to be made and innumerable losses.

In her sadness, Lynnie began devising ways to end her life. She rehearsed the plans over in her mind, but something stopped her. "I didn't want to hurt this little baby! It wasn't his fault I was such a mess."

She had gone to church. She had read the Bible. She had a great family. "My mom is the greatest! Without my family, I don't know where I would be," Lynnie beams. "But I was selfish and defiant," she adds. "God in his infinite wisdom used a little baby boy to get my attention."

After her son Dustin was born, Lynnie married Phil, and they have a great love story. Phil fell head over heels for Lynnie as well as for her busy 1-year-old. Four children later, Phil and Lynnie still play footsie on the couch and make me blush with their sweetness.

Today Lynnie ministers to young women in all kinds of situations. She has a passionate message of hope for girls in trouble. "God is in control and nothing happens that he doesn't know about. He provides. He restores. He is the one to turn to in crisis. He gives new life because he wants everyone to be saved and know the truth, and he will forgive any sin we've committed if we ask. He can make you a new creation."

There was a time when it was downright impossible for Lynnie to see a happy ending to her story. Sometimes when a girl bravely chooses what is right for the sake of a tiny one, she finds herself knee-deep in disapproval, heartbreak, fear, and loneliness. She'll cash in times of carefree play for a hard-to-swallow dose of extra-adulthood. But there are some blessings she can find only when she is courageous. They come trickling in at first, barely noticed, and then come gushing in at unexpected moments!

God, in his artistry, uses the hard stuff (failures, unthinkable challenges) to mold some into heart-and-soul people, Phil and Lynnie folk—those golden few who have turned adversity into transformation.

The genealogies that map out the path to Christ are peppered with people who entered the world under shady circumstances, and some who made grave mistakes. Even Jesus as a boy must have known what it was like to live under a swirl of suspicion and speculation about exactly how he came to be. I guess God knows just what we feel and has an uncanny ability to work things out. To God, failures are opportunities.

I wish I could have been there for my friend years ago in her time of crisis. I would be out of breath talking so fast, anxious to tell her how happy her life would someday be. "Take heart," I'd say. "God has a great idea for you and will take care of you and your baby in ways you haven't thought of."

I would challenge her to be brave, to face one day at a time, and to be proud of her decision to bring a life into the world. There isn't any accomplishment she could achieve in life to match such a wonder. I would promise my friendship and prayer and tell her just how proud I am that she made a decision everyone can *live* with.

SCRIPTURE HELP

+ **Deuteronomy 31:6**
+ **Psalm 32:1-7**
+ **Psalm 46**
+ **Psalm 116:5-7**
+ **Psalm 121**

+ **Psalm 139:13-16**
+ **Isaiah 43:18-19**
+ **Jeremiah 1:5**
+ **Ephesians 2:4-10**
+ **Hebrews 12:1-3**

Care and Counseling Tips

THE BASICS

Teenagers are working on figuring out how they fit into the world around them. They are asking questions such as, "Who am I?" "Who do I want to be?" "Do I have what it takes to become that kind of person?" Students are making their own decisions—deciding what friends to spend time with or what activities to be involved in. Some are becoming involved in intimate relationships—an area confusing even to adults. It's a major challenge for young people, these not-quite adults, to navigate the turbulent waters of dating relationships. A teenager's fragile heart deeply feels the sting of rejection and the ache of being unwanted.

Society does not help us as we work to guide teenagers toward sexual purity. It views abstinence as an archaic idea. In some settings, people hand students free condoms and tell them that they are incapable of controlling their urges. Young people today are catapulted into an adult world for which they are emotionally unprepared.

This chapter discusses the all-too-common problems of teenage pregnancy and abortion. An unexpected pregnancy will change the course of a teenager's life forever, regardless of how she responds to her situation. Another challenge many teenagers face is post-abortion stress. Teen mothers often make choices out of fear—choices they come to regret. The issues of unexpected pregnancy and abortion have significant impacts on the heart of a teenager. Those closest to the young woman—including you as her youth leader—need to know how to address these issues effectively and compassionately.

Care Tips

A teenager has just taken a home pregnancy test. It's positive. She tells you she doesn't know what to do; she feels paralyzed. Everybody else seems to have an opinion. You have the opportunity to speak truth to the teenager and help calm her fears so that she can make a clear decision. But how do you do this?

✚ Listen.

Many young women don't have anyone in their lives who will simply listen. So just listen until she asks you for advice. Once a young woman knows that you are listening to her, your words will have greater impact.

✚ Ask about pressures and fears.

Find out what her pressures are (parents, boyfriend, finances, reputation) and the impact that each of these people or circumstances has on her life. Having her name her fears will also take away some of their power—talking about fears with a compassionate listener often helps to lessen them.

✚ Help her identify feelings.

Crises bring up many emotions for teenagers. Listen as she expresses feelings other than fear, such as guilt, dread, isolation, and loss.

✚ Ask about family.

Explore the topic of family reactions with your student. If she has not told her parents or other trusted adults yet, offer to go with her to do so. Help her prepare for their initial reaction.

✚ Make a connection.

If one of your teenagers is facing an unplanned pregnancy, contact a local crisis pregnancy center, which is a pro-life agency that will help her through the crisis. (See the "Additional Resources" section for the Web site for Option Line, an organization that will connect you with crisis pregnancy centers in your area).

WHEN TO REFER

+ When the pregnancy is the result of rape or incest
+ When the student displays signs of depression (see Chapter 2, "Depression")
+ When the student displays signs of suicidal tendencies (see Chapter 3, "Suicide")
+ When the student displays destructive behavior, such as an eating disorder; cutting, scratching, or burning herself; excessive drug or alcohol use; or indiscriminate sex
+ When the student has had an abortion in the past

Counseling Tips

God did not design the female heart to have to make a decision about whether to end the life of her child. Yet today's teenagers live in a society where abortion has been legal since before they were born. A teenager's decision to have an abortion can leave her with a train wreck of emotions. Look for these symptoms of post-abortion stress:

+ **Avoidance of any person or situation that could trigger painful emotions related to the pregnancy**
+ **Preoccupation with becoming pregnant again**
+ **Fear of being infertile**
+ **Increase in symptoms around the anniversary of the abortion or due date of the baby**
+ **Development of unhealthy eating habits**
+ **Sudden or unexplainable bouts of crying**

You can help a teenager who has had an abortion by connecting her to group or individual Christian counseling. Crisis pregnancy centers are great resources for this. Group counseling can be healing for a young woman as she talks with others who know what she has been through. You can also talk to the student about finding safe people to share her secret with. Be aware that the teenager is likely working through the cycle of grief (see Chapter 1, "Grief"). It may be helpful for her to memorialize her child's life somehow, such as giving her child a name, making something for the child, or taking a trip to a local memorial for unborn babies.

Group Tips

If a teenager in your ministry is experiencing a crisis pregnancy, enlist the support of the whole group in the following ways:

+ Get the group involved.
Challenge your youth group to gather information from Web sites and organizations devoted to nurturing women in crisis pregnancies. Engage them in ministry. Ask them to bring helpful information they might find about support options available to teen parents, encouraging thoughts, and Bible verses.

+ Create a Friendship Contract.
As a group, create a contract friends can sign to pledge love, prayer support, and lasting friendship to one another. Keep the points realistic to avoid setting everyone up for failure. Each person signing the contract should include a phone number or e-mail address they can be reached at when someone in the group needs a listening ear.

+ Enlist the Prayer Force.
If you sense your youth group is talking about the teenager or the situation in a negative way, ask them specifically to pray their friend through this rocky time, individually and as a group. It's hard to belittle someone you are praying for.

+ Host a Worry-Free Fun Fest!
Invite everyone to an evening of junk food and board games. The ticket of admission is an index card with their worries written on it. Collect the cards at the door, placing them in a secure trash bucket or shredder. For the next few hours, give kids the permission to have worry-free fun, with no thought of what is burdening them.

+ Be a friend before and after the baby is born.

If your student decides to keep and raise her baby, brainstorm ways the group can help—a baby shower, baby-sitting, unconditional friendship. In the months that follow, invite her to do fun things with the group or with individuals, arranging child care if necessary.

ADDITIONAL RESOURCES

+ Books

Equipped to Serve: Caring for Women in Crisis Pregnancies. Fourth Edition. Cynthia R. Philkill and Suzanne Walsh. Sparta, MI: Frontlines Publishing, 1999.

A Season to Heal. Luci Freed and Penny Yvonne Salazar. Nashville, TN: Cumberland House Publishing, 1993.

+ Online Resources

www.care-net.org (Care Net)

www.optionline.org (Option Line)

What Not to Say

+"What are you going to do?"

It's overwhelming to try and have all of the answers at this point. Your friend needs to work through her pregnancy one day at a time. Instead, pray with her for wisdom.

+ "Everyone makes mistakes."

This might wrongly imply that the baby is a mistake. Psalm 127:3 teaches that children are a reward from God. If your friend feels convicted about past sin, take her to Psalm 51 and help her find healing in God's forgiveness.

+ "We're all here for you."

Chances are, as the months roll on, many of her friends will resume their normal youthful activities. She will feel more alone than ever. Give her a phone number she can call when she needs you. (Male youth sponsors may be more comfortable introducing her to a female role model.) Remind her that she has a friend who "sticks closer than a brother" in Christ (Proverbs 18:24).

What to Say

+ "Let's just take this one day at a time."

Celebrate the small milestones and don't expect her to be able to digest everything at once. Help her get through this challenge 24 hours at a time.

+ "You can do this."

God promises the strength we need to do the right thing. Empower your teenager by believing in her heartily. Offer hope, reminding her that God is a kind Father. He is in control and very near.

+ "I will always be your friend."

Give your student the security of knowing you love her, despite mistakes, trouble, and periods of un-fun. This will go a long way in helping her understand the miracle of God's grace.

+ "What have you decided to name the baby?"

During the later stages of pregnancy, if your student decides to raise the baby, choose encouraging comments and questions. Help your teenager get excited about the birth of her precious little one.

FOR GUYS ONLY

With so much attention being focused on the young woman, the baby's father can sometimes be overlooked. It's often best if a young man talks with a male counselor. He may be experiencing a profound sense of helplessness if others are leaving him out of important decisions. You can help by listening and assuring him you will stick by him. Encourage his involvement in this time of crisis, but help him sort out his responsibilities and establish boundaries. This is a teachable moment in which you can help a young man learn a great deal about integrity and responsibility in relationships.

If both the young man and woman are in your group and plan to continue their relationship, consider connecting them with a mentor couple, who can walk them through their changing relationship and give parenting tips along the way.

CHAPTER EIGHT

Academic Problems
Assisting Students With School Struggles

with counseling insights from **D. PATRICK HOPP, PH.D.**
+ ministry tips from **JAMES W. MILLER**

I can't say I blame them. It was only a matter of time before I got the boot from the private school my parents were spending so much money to send me to. Now I've got to transfer to a public school with no friends and this on my record. It's like being a freshman again. I'm sure my teachers will all know about me before I get there.

It's not like I didn't want to get good grades. I tried. Or I guess I tried to try. I just couldn't focus. When I knew things were going downhill in math, I tried to compensate by working extra hard in my other classes. Then when chemistry started going the same way, I just couldn't keep my head above water. It was like, even in art class, which I really liked, all I could do was think about how bad I was doing in math and chemistry.

Then I'd get home in the evenings, and I was so depressed that I couldn't concentrate on my homework. I'd get halfway through a set of problems and realize I had no idea what I was doing. I hadn't understood what the teacher was saying in class, and I didn't to draw attention to myself, so I just sat there. Now I was lost. I also didn't want to tick my parents off, so I couldn't go downstairs and announce that I wasn't doing my homework because I couldn't. C's turned into zeros. I just stopped turning stuff in.

When the final exams came back, I didn't even look at mine until I got to my locker, and even then I didn't look any farther than the fraction at the top. A grade of 23 out of 100. Is that even possible?

So now it's a done deal. They had warned me before and I had made promises I couldn't keep. There was nowhere to go but right out the front door. Public school, at least, should be easier, but I feel even less motivated to work now. The whole thing is an embarrassment.

The guys at church seem to care about me, but school isn't really what they do. I mean, they always care about how I feel, and they paid a lot of attention when I told them about the fights I was getting in with my parents because of my grades, but it's not like they're a tutoring service or anything. I don't really need someone to just pat me on the head this time. I really need help. I don't know how to get motivated or how to get my work done.

I also think it's unfair that you get judged on grades alone. When I'm out riding my bike, I have all kinds of thoughts about deep things that I had never thought of before. When I'm free from the classroom, my mind opens up to all kinds of ideas. I feel like I could learn so much better if we only moved the class outside. But I feel like the message I'm getting is that you can only pass if you can learn in a claustrophobic atmosphere. I'm not dumb—I just can't take tests on hard desks in small rooms with all kinds of noise. When my friends and I went camping for a weekend, we had some of the best conversations I've ever had. It was like we were learning from each other. But again, no points on the SAT for that.

I want to be an architect. That way, I can be outside on work sites and do nothing but draw my ideas into reality. I know there are jobs I could totally do, but why do I have to read *A Tale of Two Cities* in order to be able to do that?

My parents are both taking it completely differently. My mom comes down hard on me and practically yells at me every day. Good motivation, Mom. Now I'm inspired. Dad always found school easy and has no idea why I can't do it. When you're the super-successful business manager, you don't have to pay too much attention to the underachiever you've raised. You just go back to work. Also not inspiring.

So here I am, sitting at my desk again—that is, what I can see of it under piles of papers that I never turned in and books that I'm not going to read. In a dark room. Sheesh. This place is a dump. Note to self: Clean room after getting straight A's. Equally likely.

Just got a phone call from Gina at church. A bunch of them apparently want to come over for a study session in algebra. They said it didn't matter that we weren't in the same class, because the subject is the same wherever you learn it. Sweet! More important, Gina is coming over.

Would love to write more, but I have T minus 10 minutes to clean up this dive. Who would have thought math would be my favorite thing to do?

WHEN TO REFER

There are serious problems that can inhibit students' academic performance. If you see symptoms of the following problems, talk to the family about involving other professionals. A psychologist or other mental health professional can assess the situation and make appropriate treatment recommendations.

+ Learning Disabilities: Difficulty following directions, frequent reversal of letters or numbers, difficulty learning new concepts or making connections between concepts, consistent reading or spelling errors, difficulty with eye-hand coordination

+ Attention-Deficit Disorder: Distractibility, forgetfulness, disorganization, restlessness, impulsivity

+ Depression: (see Chapter 2, "Depression")

+ Anxiety Disorders: (see Chapter 10, "Stress and Anxiety")

+ Substance Abuse: (see Chapter 4, "Addictions")

Care and Counseling Tips

THE BASICS

We all know what it's like to occasionally lack motivation in some area of our lives. We've sat at our desks and stared at a computer screen or walked by a pile of laundry, waiting for a better time to get started on it. But for some students, procrastination and apathy go beyond these momentary motivational dry spells into a desert in which any attempt to get started seems to end in a disappointing mirage. These students are often bright and capable—their academic struggles do not stem from a lack of intelligence or ambition—but they cannot seem to break free from the burdens that weigh them down and keep them from reaching their academic potential. Perhaps the most common obstacles come from within:

+ Self-Perception
Many students struggle from obstacles they've placed in their own minds. Students who believe they're not good at math problems will perform at a lower level than students who believe they will excel.

+ Fear of Failure
A fear of failure motivates some students more than a desire to succeed. For example, students who study because they're afraid of disappointing their parents are bound to do worse than those motivated by a desire to do well.

+ Internal Incentives
Students tend to do better work when internal incentives (the desire to learn or an interest in the subject matter) rather than external incentives (the desire for good grades or approval) are motivating them. Top-performing students are genuinely fascinated by what they are learning.

Care Tips

If it appears that a student is having problems:

+ Don't be afraid to ask.

Find out if the student is having difficulties by asking simple, direct, and matter-of-fact questions. For example, "How's school going for you?" or "It seems like you feel overwhelmed by the amount of homework you have." Lead into the questions by stating that you care about the student and want to know what is happening in his or her life.

+ Don't minimize the problem.

The student has probably already been told that he or she just needs to work harder or isn't really applying him or herself. This creates even more pressure that could lead to anxiety or procrastination. Instead, continue asking questions to fully understand the situation.

+ Help create a positive academic self-image.

Look for small successes, and then find out what the student did to excel. What did it feel like to succeed? Help him or her visualize future successes.

Counseling Tips

To continue to support the student in long-term academic success, try these tips:

+ Discover the student's interests.
Find subjects that the student enjoys or excels at and build on them. The teenager needs to begin to see himself or herself as a person who is capable of academic success.

+ Meet a professor.
Arrange a meeting with a professor in a nearby college. You can probably find a willing teacher who can impress upon a young person how important learning has been in his or her life. Most professors would probably be flattered by this unique use of an office hour.

+ Provide study tips.
Sometimes teenagers need help in developing good study skills. If the opportunity arises, share with the student the techniques that worked for you in school. For example, helping the student get organized and plan assignments can go a long way.

Group Tips

+ Try a study group in your ministry.

If you find that several students are having similar problems with organization or specific subjects, organize a study group. Provide an atmosphere that is free from distraction. Decide if you can make tutoring available during that time. Or just model some new study techniques, like making flashcards or quizzing games.

+ Take a museum tour that makes study interesting.

Sometimes the challenge to study is that it seems dull and drab. Modern museums have often caught on to this idea and go out of the way to invest in more curious presentations. Some science museums have creative presentations that allow people to get physically involved in the displays. Take your group on a weekend excursion.

+ Have a decorating party.

An important part of study is a work space that is clean and free from distraction. Take some time to decorate a room together, maybe even after a shopping spree. Create a space that is clean, pleasant, and free from distraction. When a young person is proud of his or her room, he or she is more likely to use it for study.

+ Teach a self-reward system.

It's good to learn that you can "reward yourself" when you accomplish things you set out to do. Encourage all of your students to plan a certain reward for their academic accomplishments, whether it be an ice cream sundae, a trip to the mall, or a weekend camping trip.

What Not to Say

+ "It's not that important."

You don't want to minimize the importance of education and study. Instead, you want to encourage the ongoing process of learning, even if it is at a speed appropriate to the learner.

+ "Lots of people were successful without finishing college."

This actually avoids a number of important issues. Someone with academic problems is sensitive about their abilities. This comment doesn't encourage them.

+ "You'll be good at other things."

This is just giving up. Instead, you want to encourage persistence and patience that will pay off in the long run. If the student gets the impression that the situation is hopeless, the student will lose hope.

What to Say

+ "You can develop a learning style that works best for you."

In fact, people do learn in different ways. Some are auditory, some visual, some kinetic. Young people can improve their study skills by learning which style works best for them.

+ "God gave you your mind."

It's important to know that God made us and God can use us for his purposes. That knowledge will encourage a young person to keep working at it and not give up.

+ "Your worth as a person can't be measured."

One big issue with academic challenges is self-esteem. The person involved needs to know that his or her value isn't on the line. Emphasizing the importance of study should never equate to a person's self-worth.

+ "Struggle happens to everyone. Quitting only happens to quitters."

Students can learn through this process that struggle isn't fatal and doesn't bring an end to their hard work. Struggle can be a fertile training ground for God to use.

ADDITIONAL RESOURCES

+ Books

How to Study. Sixth Edition. Ron Fry. Clifton Park, NY: Thompson Delmar Learning, 2005.

Study Power: Study Skills to Improve Your Learning and Your Grades. William R. Luckie and Wood Smethurst. Cambridge, MA: Brookline Books, 1998.

+ Online Resources

www.chadd.org (CHADD—Children and Adults with Attention Deficit/Hyperactivity Disorder)

www.ldanatl.org (Learning Disabilities Association of America)

www.ldonline.org (LD Online—resources and information about learning disabilities)

+ Other

Talk to learning professionals at your local high school, or seek out advice from professional learning centers or tutors.

SCRIPTURE HELP

+ **Deuteronomy 6:4-9**
+ **Psalm 119:65-66**
+ **Proverbs 2:1-6**
+ **Proverbs 3:13-15**
+ **Proverbs 24:3-5**

+ **Matthew 22:36-37**
+ **Luke 2:41-52**
+ **Romans 5:3-5**
+ **Colossians 3:17**
+ **1 Timothy 4:12**

STUDY TIPS

If you're having a hard time with some areas of schoolwork, try these tips for managing time and succeeding in school:

• Make an academic calendar. As soon as your teachers give you papers, tests, and other assignments, write down the due date on your calendar.

• Create a daily homework schedule that includes the estimated chunks of time you'll need to complete specific assignments.

• Break large assignments into smaller, more manageable tasks, and work on one piece at a time.

• Find a place to study that's free from distractions. Study there consistently, and try to use this place only for studying. This will help reduce distractions because you'll associate the place only with studying.

• Review notes and reading materials often throughout the semester rather than waiting until right before exams to cram everything into your memory.

• Try to mentally associate new material with personal experiences and things you know well. For example, what might a historical figure you're learning about have in common with the lead singer of your favorite band?

• Find creative ways to make studying more fun. Make up your own version of games such as Jeopardy! or Trivial Pursuit to learn the material for your classes.

CHAPTER NINE

Family Conflict

Overcoming Communication Challenges
Between Teenagers and Their Families

with counseling insights from **TERRI S. WATSON, PSY.D.**
+ ministry tips from **JAMES W. MILLER AND FRED WHAPLES**

Counselor: OK, why don't we slow down a little bit and I'll have each of you explain exactly what you saw happen and how you felt about…

Janet: My mom went crazy is what happened. I'm so serious. So I'm walking out of the movie theater…

Mom: That you weren't supposed to be at.

Janet: Don't interrupt!

Mom: Don't yell!

Janet: Don't interrupt! So anyway, I come walking out with my friends and my mom has been completely stalking me! She's sitting there outside the theater hiding in a phone booth.

Mom: I needed to make a phone call.

Janet: You have a cell!

Mom: The battery was dying.

Janet: Mom! You jumped on me coming out of the movie in front of all my friends and totally went crazy!

Mom: Well, you told me you were going to Belinda's house for Bible study, and when I called Belinda's house, her mom told me you all had gone to the movie, and there was never any Bible study at all.

Janet: That's because you never let me do anything unless it's at church, and I don't want to spend my life withering away at church! It's embarrassing that whenever my friends ask if I can go out, I always have to go to choir practice or something!

Mom: Richard, tell your daughter she's grounded…

Dad: Leave me outta this.

Mom: …and that she can't go to Belinda's house ever again or have a cell.

Janet: Mom, that's totally unfair. You'll just change your mind tomorrow anyway.

Counselor: Well now! That was quite a lot to go through. Let me check in on a couple of details. Janet, as best you can, I want you to tell me what you think your mother was feeling when she first heard from your friend's mother that you weren't at a Bible study.

Janet: I don't know.

Counselor: Well, think about it for a minute. Have you ever had a friend tell you one thing and do something else?

Janet: I guess.

Counselor: Well, Sandy, let me ask you first then. What went through your daughter's head when she walked out of the theater and saw you there?

Mom: That she was nabbed.

Counselor: And what else?

Mom: Embarrassed.

Counselor: That's my sense, too. In fact, she used that word. Does Janet have the freedom to do things outside of church activities?

Mom: Well, when I was her age I got into all kinds of trouble, and I wish someone had been there to prevent it. My parents were reckless.

Counselor: Do you wish someone had just controlled you, or taught you to make good decisions?

Mom: Well, obviously the latter, but maybe some of both.

Counselor: Fair enough. In my experience, though, children who are controlled often act like children who have no boundaries. Janet, I want to get back to you. Now that you've had some time, how do you think your mom felt on the phone with your friend's mom?

Janet: I don't know.

Counselor: I can tell you don't want to talk about it, but I'm inviting you into a new kind of relationship with your mom. You'll always be her child, but the day will come when you are two adults who have an adult relationship with each other. I'm trying to invite you to the beginnings of that relationship.

Janet: (Remains silent.)

Counselor: That involves thinking seriously about how the other person feels.

Janet: I know, she was embarrassed; she felt like she wasn't good enough; she thought someone else might know that we weren't the perfect little family.

Counselor: Sandy, does she have that right?

Mom: We don't need to be perfect. I just want to know that I can trust you.

Janet: What have I done that you can't trust me? I mean, before this.

Mom: It's not just you, Janet. It's what happens to teenagers. I know.

Counselor: Richard, what are your thoughts?

Dad: You shouldn't lie to your mother. Just do what you're told and we can avoid all of this.

Counselor: Can your wife and daughter talk to you about their conflicts?

Dad: Sure.

Mom and Janet: No!

Dad: I'm busy.

Counselor: Well, be that as it may, if you wanted to, you might play a key role in giving them an outlet just by listening to them. It might help them think through their relationship just to be able to bounce their thoughts off you.

Dad: OK.

Counselor: Janet, I don't hear that your mom wants to distrust you. It sounds like she has had experiences of her own that make her expect that she's not going to be able to trust you. You might not be used to thinking about it this way, but you can help her through that as you go through your teen years.

Janet: How?

Counselor: By showing her that you won't abuse a little independence.

Mom: That would mean a lot to me. Of course, if you abuse it, then you are grounded until you are 18.

Janet: Mom!

Counselor: (Sighs.)

SCRIPTURE HELP

+ **Joshua 24:15**
+ **Nehemiah 4:14**
+ **Psalm 139:13-16**
+ **Lamentations 3:31-33**
+ **John 11:17-44**

+ **Romans 5:1-5**
+ **Romans 8:35-39**
+ **2 Corinthians 4:6-12**
+ **Philippians 2:1-11**
+ **Philippians 3:10-14**

Care and Counseling Tips

THE BASICS

It's particularly important for families to have good communication during their children's teenage years. Active parent-adolescent communication can have a preventative effect on a number of serious teenage problems, including drug and alcohol abuse, academic problems, and teenage pregnancy. Adolescents who can "talk out" their problems and concerns are less likely to "act out." Adolescents who are able to assertively express their needs to others are less likely to be aggressive. And most important, healthy family communication can enhance a teenager's spiritual development.

You have the opportunity to play a key role in helping students and families keep the channels of communication open. You can also help teach families conflict resolution skills.

There are several barriers to communication:

• Some parents fear that open communication and negotiation will undermine their authority. Not so! Two-way communication increases teenagers' respect for their parents and increases compliance.

• Other parents feel they cannot say no and don't take enough of a position of authority.

• Many families are unable to deal with the expression of negative feelings such as hurt, anger, and disappointment. They might "tiptoe" around each other and avoid addressing the underlying reasons for tension in the family.

Care Tips

When you are counseling a teenager and his or her family, use these guidelines:

+ Involve both parents and teenagers.
Adopt a family perspective in your counseling. Everyone will need to be involved in defining problems and creating solutions.

+ Identify strengths.
All families bring unique abilities to the art of communication, including humor, tact, or strong mutual caring. Find these strengths, and help the family use them in times of conflict.

+ Maintain neutrality.
A neutral third party can offer much assistance to parents and teenagers who are stuck in conflict. Avoid placing blame, and focus on the communication style as the problem, rather than a particular person. Also, while you may feel an alliance with the student, it's important not to undermine parental authority.

+ Reframe the problem.
Help the family look at the situation in a different way. For example, "Jonny has just become so rebellious" can be restated in a more positive light as "Jonny is trying to be more independent."

Counseling Tips

Here are some ongoing issues to consider when working with families:

+ Prevention.
Consider providing parent education and support classes in your church where parents can explore characteristics of good parent-child communication. Helping parents identify potential communication blocks early on can prevent the development of more serious conflicts down the road.

+ Mentoring.
For a family that's gridlocked in conflict, consider assigning a mentor family in the church. Ask the parents of each family to meet with the opposite teenager. This can help the family in conflict gain a new perspective and pick up some practical ideas from the mentor family.

+ Rituals.
Family rituals that allow members to air conflicts and concerns as a part of everyday life can be helpful—such rituals could include family meetings, dinnertime conversations, or weekly check-ins with each child. Families can prevent the buildup of conflict and resentment by planning a regular outlet.

Group Tips

+ Stay neutral.

Never allow your group or leaders to side with anyone in a family conflict. Instead, all outside parties must stay neutral and try to mediate both sides to an appropriate resolution. If one side is clearly inappropriate, then you may move that particular family member more aggressively to the right decision by highlighting differing views and facts that you have personally observed, but maintain neutrality.

+ Be a supportive community.

Allow time for students to share candidly with one another, and have them support and pray specifically for those needs. You should not limit this to just a small group (such as a home fellowship or a cell group) activity but should do this regularly in every possible platform. Let your students carry one another's burdens and hear similar struggles. This will create community and will keep you informed about the issues your students are facing.

+ Have resources and trainings readily available for the family.

The number one influence on a student's life is his or her parents. We must have resources readily available to meet the challenges and opportunities parents face as their kids are becoming adults. Have a "Family Resource Center" in your office or youth space filled with books, videos, trainings, and articles that parents can check out to help them in their successful navigation of family issues. You can also host parenting-type classes and discussion groups.

+ Host family events.

As a group, make sure to have some specific times when you include the entire family in your events. Don't just focus on your students, but intentionally create an atmosphere where families experience an activity and are then equipped to purposely discuss, interact with, and apply the lessons learned.

Some parents are hesitant to plug into the student ministry when their kids are involved, thinking it would be uncomfortable for their kids if they're present. The fact is, students need to have their parents intricately involved in their faith, and you need parental influence to work toward the faith you are instilling in your students for the greatest success and lifelong impact.

WHEN TO REFER

Some degree of conflict is normal, and even healthy, in families with teenagers. However, it's important for you to recognize when the conflict places a student at risk for more serious emotional and behavioral problems. The following situations warrant a referral to a licensed marriage and family therapist or mental health professional:

+ **The family conflict is interfering with the normal adjustment of the teenager (such as affecting school work, relationships, or a job).**
+ **The student makes references to behaviors such as running away, substance abuse, physical violence, or suicidal thoughts.**
+ **A teenager has a long history of defiance of authority or acting-out behaviors.**
+ **The student's symptoms include sadness, mood swings, anxiety, or shame.**
+ **Emotionally or physically abusive behavior exists.**

What Not to Say

+ "Your parents are stupid."

Never side with one person in a family conflict. Even if one party's approach seems correct, it is more important that you stay neutral and assist in resolving the conflict. To side with your student would mean undermining the parent; never give the impression that the parent has done something wrong or inappropriate in a family conflict.

+ "Your teenager needs to submit to your authority."

Again, stay neutral. To side with the parent would mean undermining the relationship you are building with your student.

+ "Shut up!"

Even though some conflicts seem petty or blown out of proportion, work to create an atmosphere where open and safe discussion happens and where real listening takes place.

+ "You should just move out. If you need a place to go, you can stay with me."

Running away from issues is never the answer, and neither is having a minor out on the streets or living with you. The greatest thing you can do as a youth leader is to bring the family together. If resolution seems impossible, professionals should become involved.

What to Say

+ "Let's talk."

The first step is to open the lines of communication between you and the family. Visit them in the home, invite them over for dinner, or go to a restaurant. Talk about life, activities, struggles, joys, and the conflict they are facing. Let the family really open up and listen for places of sensitivity. Stay quiet and do not offer advice until you have clearly heard all the issues involved.

+ "What can we all agree on?"

Find the common ground for the family. Find out where the negotiable points are and, even if they seem minor, make them a tool for mediation. Help family members create peace by finding what they all agree on.

+ "How are you doing now?"

Once you have heard of or assisted in a family conflict resolution, make sure to follow up on the issue. Keep notes on the conflict and check up with all parties of the family over several months to make certain the conflict is not still a point of contention. Make sure the resolution is still applying and working. Let the family know your care, concern, and partnership is genuine and not just based on the immediate issues.

ADDITIONAL RESOURCES

+ Books

Angry Kids: Understanding and Managing the Emotions That Control Them. Richard L. Berry. Grand Rapids, MI: Fleming H. Revell Co., 2001.

The Family: A Christian Perspective on the Contemporary Home. Second Edition. Jack O. Balswick and Judith K. Balswick. Grand Rapids, MI: Baker Books, 1999.

Resolving Conflict. Josh McDowell and Ed Stewart. Nashville, TN: W Publishing Group, 2000.

+ Online Resources

www.family.org (Focus on the Family)

Stress and Anxiety
Ministering to Stressed-Out Students

with counseling insights from
SCOTT GIBSON, M.S.W., L.C.S.W.
+ ministry tips from SIV M. RICKETTS

Marcos was a high school junior when he felt his life spin out of his control. On the surface everything looked great: He was getting decent grades in honors and advanced placement classes; he was a starter on the school soccer team and could hold his own on the guitar; he served as a leader in his church youth group; his parents' marriage seemed fine; the family had enough money; and Marcos had plenty of friends both at school and church.

But inside Marcos felt like at any moment he might just break and let out a giant-sized scream. Marcos moved from one activity to the next with little or no time in between and definitely no time to rest. He regularly fell into bed after midnight and still had to get up before 6 a.m. He rarely had time to sit down and enjoy dinner with his family but had to eat quickly and dash off. And though he liked everything he did, he never felt happy. All the joy had seeped out of his activities, and worse, his life.

On those nights when Marcos actually got to bed at a decent time, he would lie awake for hours worrying. What if he didn't get into college?

What if he got into the wrong college, chose the wrong major, got a job he hated, and his whole life was a waste? What if he never met the "right" girl? Were his friends mad at him? How about global issues? Would there be a world worth living in by the time he grew up? Sometimes his heart raced and he struggled to breathe normally. He wondered if maybe something was wrong with him that he couldn't keep up the pace.

The thing was, as he looked around, Marcos saw a lot of people just as stressed out as he was. His parents poured themselves into their jobs. His friends stressed about class projects and tests, extracurricular activities, relationships, college and the future—all the same things that concerned Marcos. When Marcos tried to talk about how he was feeling, he just as often got a list of what everyone else was anxious about. Was anybody happy?

Marcos watched as some of his friends tried drugs, mostly pot or drinking. They said it helped them relax and blow off steam after an intense week. Marcos felt tempted but didn't think that would solve anything. Too much potential for even worse problems. His church friends, who seemed just as busy and stressed out as he felt, said, "Oh, God will take care of it. Just pray and you'll be fine." But it didn't seem to be working for them. In fact, church added another whole layer of activities: Sunday morning worship, midweek youth group, service projects—all good things but sometimes they seemed like just more to do. Where was God in all this?

Marcos knew this couldn't be how God intended life to be, but he didn't see an alternative. Just as he began to resign himself to enduring rather than enjoying life, his small group leader invited him out for a soda and Marcos, feeling desperate, found time to fit it into his crazy schedule.

He asked me how I was doing and he listened. But then he asked how I was feeling. He wanted to know, beyond the list of activities I juggle, how I was managing personally: emotionally and spiritually. He didn't judge me. He didn't try to fix me. He listened. No one had listened to me that way in, oh, I can't remember how long. I felt exhausted just from talking about everything. I mean, I really dumped all over him. And he took it.

Marcos' small group leader asked if he could read a passage from the

Bible: Matthew 6:25-34. Without judgment, he affirmed that Marcos was right, that God didn't intend for people to worry so much. God loves us and cares for us in ways we too seldom acknowledge. He asked Marcos if he would like to meet again so they could talk about time management skills and see if they could help Marcos better manage his activities and his anxiety. He also encouraged Marcos to have his parents make him an appointment with a medical doctor, who would check that Marcos was physically healthy and help determine whether Marcos' worrying was part of an anxiety disorder that would require treatment.

Marcos walked away from that meeting with a new and surprising feeling: hope. Someone had noticed and truly cared about him. Someone had pointed him beyond the urgent needs pressing in on him, threatening to drown him, to a better way of living.

A few weeks later, with a clean bill of health from a doctor (the doctor applauded Marcos' courage for being honest and seeking a better quality of life), Marcos and his small group leader met again. They prayed. They read the Bible. They made a list of everything Marcos did each day. They talked about changes Marcos could make and activities he could cut which, though it would be hard, would make Marcos happier in the long run. They scheduled in time for fun and relaxation. They talked about people they knew who might be good examples of living a balanced life and how Marcos might get to know a few new friends who would help him grow in this area. They set a regular appointment for every three weeks to talk and pray specifically about things that were causing Marcos stress and anxiety.

At first, some people experienced shock as Marcos set about making changes. His parents and school counselor were concerned when, at the beginning of the semester, he decided not to take an advanced placement class many of his friends would take. But Marcos knew he'd need extra time to study for the other advanced placement tests, so he took a slightly easier course in order to free up time. His youth pastor was disappointed when Marcos decided he wouldn't serve as a student leader, though he would continue to play in the worship band. The youth pastor was gracious though, recognizing that Marcos would be a healthier person and a healthier Christian. Of course, Marcos would still be a leader in the ministry whether or not he attended leadership meetings. Marcos made soccer a priority because he needed the outlet of exercise. And, besides, it was fun—another new priority. He also set aside at least five minutes a day—no matter what!—to read his Bible and talk to God, something he knew would help him keep his life in perspective.

SCRIPTURE HELP

+ **Deuteronomy 31:8**
+ **Psalm 27:1**
+ **Psalm 94:18-19**
+ **Psalm 139:23-24**
+ **Proverbs 12:25**

+ **Matthew 6:25-34**
+ **John 14:27**
+ **Philippians 3:12-14**
+ **Philippians 4:4-9**
+ **1 Peter 5:6-7**

Care and Counseling Tips

THE BASICS

Every one of us experiences stress. Short-term stress can help us prepare to be at our very best. Before taking final exams, many students experience anxiety that helps them get ready for the challenge ahead. They may experience nervousness in their stomach, sweaty palms, increased heart rate, and increased blood pressure.

However, a constant state of stress can be physically and psychologically damaging. When students don't handle stress or handle it poorly, problems such as high blood pressure, ulcers, or other conditions can result. Many teenagers today encounter stress from several sources: Their bodies are changing rapidly, they feel pressured to succeed in school, they're involved in unpredictable peer relationships, and they're trying to renegotiate family relationships.

You're probably already aware of many of the stressors your students encounter, but you can help them learn to handle their stress in healthy ways.

Care Tips

The first step in helping your student reduce stress is to help him or her identify where the stress is coming from. It may be obvious to you, but it's important that the student be able to recognize the source for him or herself. This will greatly aid the student in problem solving and dealing with stress in the future. To simplify the process, you might help him or her categorize the situation into external and internal stressors:

✛ External stressors.

Often an external event creates stress in a student's life. Some examples might include a divorce, a relationship with a boyfriend or girlfriend, a family's relocation to a new area, or a school problem. Some external sources of stress students can change and others they can't. If it seems that the student could have a part in changing the situation, ask open-ended questions like "It seems that if there were a way to do it differently, that would be nice for you. What do you think?" If not, help the teenager accept the situation and adapt to it.

✛ Internal stressors.

Internal stressors relate to how we think and feel about the everyday events in our lives. Beliefs such as "I'll do horribly at this activity," "people won't understand," or "nothing will help" all create greater stress when dealing with everyday problems. The good news about internal stressors is that we can change them. Try having your student journal every night before bed. Many internal stressors seem less important when seen on paper.

Counseling Tips

Demonstrate to your anxious students the following techniques:

+ Teach relaxation and calming techniques.
People can use a number of techniques to relax and calm themselves. Teach your teenager about visualization (imagining a more peaceful place), distraction (engaging in physical activities when stressed), deep breathing, and muscle relaxation (tightening and relaxing muscle groups). Check out the box on page 124 of this chapter for muscle relaxation ideas.

+ Encourage journaling.
Research has shown that expressing emotions in writing is an effective way to help people psychologically deal with different problems.

+ Encourage prayer.
People with stress and anxiety problems need to know that God is listening and is able to deliver them from any problem. Although God doesn't always deliver them in the way they had in mind, the process of prayer can still be very calming.

+ Recognize unrealistic thinking and expectations.
The cause of upsetting emotions is not so much the events in our lives, but how we think about those events. For example, one person accepts that a traffic jam, while frustrating, is beyond his control; another person, seeing the same traffic jam, yells, curses, and gets his blood pressure up. Thinking positively about situations can help reduce stress.

Group Tips

+ Establish prayer partners (or trios, or quads, or small groups).

Schedule a regular time when groups can get together specifically to share and pray for things that have students stressed out and anxious. Then remind students to let go and let God.

+ Sprinkle surprises.

Kind words and gestures can sure brighten a day. Have your group write notes of encouragement and mail them (who doesn't like getting snail mail?). Include uplifting Bible verses and/or short prayers of support. Bake cookies for your stressed-out friend (carrot sticks also make good stress-busting munchies). Leave a flower on your friend's doorstep. Use sidewalk chalk to write a positive message on his or her driveway. Your creativity is the limit!

+ Talk about relationships.

Relational conflict can be a major source of stress and anxiety. God is love and wants us to love one another well. Practice peacemaking and peacekeeping. Read books together on how to have healthy relationships. Talk about how to handle conflict in relationships. Make your group a safe place, where everyone can be real, honest, vulnerable, and most of all, loved.

+ Breathe.

Learn about and practice relaxation techniques. We live in a way-too-stressed-out world, and everyone feels it. Pray together. Meditate on God's Word. Practice deep breathing. Take time out to exercise, to play, to eat, to laugh, to regain perspective—God's perspective!—on life.

+ Divide up all that needs doing, and get to it.

As a group, you can learn time management techniques and help one another stick to realistic goals and tasks. Teach your students to set aside time each week (and each day, if they can) to write down what needs doing and what steps they will take to accomplish their goals. Encourage students not to worry about what they can't change and to work hard on those things they can control. Change the culture of your group from a stressed-out to a can-do crowd.

WHEN TO REFER

The following signs and symptoms may indicate that a student is experiencing too much stress and could benefit from further evaluation:

+ **Experiencing severe mood swings, withdrawing from peers, weight loss or gain, trouble in school, crying easily and often, or developing compulsive behaviors (such as hair pulling, face picking, nail biting, or excessive hand washing)**

An anxiety disorder is distinguished from normal anxiety by the intensity and frequency of the anxiety, the severity of impairment, and how long the anxiety has been a problem. A clinical diagnosis of any mental disorder is based on a number of symptoms, and only a licensed professional should make a diagnosis. The following signs may indicate an anxiety disorder:

+ **The teenager's anxiety is the result of a trauma (such as a physical or sexual assault or a car accident).**
+ **The anxiety has persisted for at least six months.**
+ **The anxiety significantly interferes with school or other major responsibilities.**
+ **Obsessions, compulsions, or panic attacks are present.**
+ **The student has suicidal thoughts.**

What Not to Say

+ "Everything will work out just fine."

This statement belittles your student's feelings. If your teenager's anxiety centers on an upcoming test, a class presentation, or a job interview, you can help your student prepare so that he or she feels more confident. Otherwise, just lending a listening ear may be all your student needs.

+ "You're such a worrywart."

First of all, what exactly is a worrywart? Has anyone ever seen one? Second, name-calling won't de-stress your teenager and may drive a wedge between you.

+ "God will take care of it."

You might as well accuse them of having no faith. And while that approach worked for Jesus, it's probably a little much for all of us mere humans. Let your students unload their concerns, and then offer to pray with them and for them.

What to Say

+ "Is there anything I can do to lighten your load?"

You can't take the exam for your student, but maybe you can quiz your student, run an errand, or bring him or her a study-break snack. Just knowing a friend cares might be help itself.

+ "If you took a 15-minute break, what could you do to have fun?"

Your student might respond with an exhausted, "But I just can't take a break!" but have the student name the fun anyway. Thinking of a few, quick fun activities might make your student laugh (or even smile) and encourage him or her to squeeze in a few minutes to relax. If you can, make the break even better by sharing the fun together.

+ "Might there be another way to look at things?"

Maybe your student tends to be a "glass is half empty" type of thinker and needs a gentle reminder that the glass is also half full. Dwelling on the negative can make the negative seem so large that it's impossible to see anything positive at all. This test might be important now, but will it really be the deciding factor on where the student goes to college? And will it matter 10 years from now? By asking questions, you can help your teenager discover the positive—and perspective—in each situation.

+ "Your identity is in God, not the things you do."

Remind your student that God's love is unconditional. Help your teenager develop an identity as a child of God and not measure his or her worth by extracurricular activities, grades, or college acceptance letters.

ADDITIONAL RESOURCES

+ Books

The Anxiety and Phobia Workbook. Edmund J. Bourne. Oakland, CA: New Harbinger Publications, Inc., 2005.

The Feeling Good Handbook. Revised Edition. David D. Burns. New York: Plume, 1990, 1999.

Life Strategies for Teens. Jay McGraw. New York: Fireside, 2000.

MUSCLE RELAXATION TECHNIQUES

Find a quiet place, and sit or lie in a comfortable position. Tense each muscle group listed below. Hold the tension and concentrate on the feeling for about 10 seconds. Then let go of the tension and concentrate on the relaxed feeling for about 10 seconds.

Face: Tighten the muscles of your face, scrunching up your face, and then relax.

Shoulders: Tighten your shoulders by raising them toward your ears, and then relax.

Chest: Take a deep breath and hold it. Notice the tension in your chest, and then let it out slowly.

Arms: Bring your lower arms up toward your shoulders, tightening the biceps, and then let your arms hang loosely.

Hands: Tighten your hands into fists, and then relax.

Stomach: Tighten your stomach muscles, and then relax.

Legs: Tighten the muscles in your upper legs by raising and holding your legs up, and then relax.

Calves: Pivoting at the ankles, pull your toes up toward your shins, and then relax.

Feet: Tighten your feet as if you were trying to make them into fists, and then relax.

CHAPTER ELEVEN

Destructive Behavior
Understanding What's
Behind Harmful Activities

with counseling insights from **KYLE D. PONTIUS, PH.D.**
+ ministry tips from **JOY-ELIZABETH F. LAWRENCE**

Susan practiced self-injury during her high school years. Currently, she is in college studying youth ministry and working as a volunteer with a youth group. About her story she said, "If my story can help one person, it's worth it."

When I was 9 years old, my parents divorced. Mom got custody of me and my older brother. The day before we learned of the divorce, my brother and I made our parents a candlelight dinner. We could tell they were having a tough time—we'd heard them fighting—but we wanted them to love each other.

For about five years afterward, I would spend every other weekend with my dad, as well as six weeks in the summer. I was totally living out of a suitcase. Both of my parents had remarried by the time I was 13. My stepdad had been a friend of the family, so that wasn't such a big deal. But my stepmom was the opposite of me. She was bossy and liked to make decisions for other people, including me. It was a messy divorce. There were money issues. My parents used me as leverage against each other. They talked bad about each other. They were mean about it.

I was so angry and frustrated about my life. My biggest question was

"Why?" Why did this happen to me? Why was no one around to walk me through this? If God would have taken on a physical form and appeared to me at that time, I'm pretty sure I would have hit him. But even so, I didn't let people see my emotions. I either hid or denied all of the negative ones.

I started cutting the summer between my freshman and sophomore year of high school. It was easy to hide it from my family. I knew that if my mother got suspicious, the first thing she'd do would be to look in my room. So I hid my stuff in other places. I was very careful to get rid of any leftover bandages or anything like that. No one could see the wounds at first because I started cutting my hips where no one would see. Honestly, hiding things from my family was really easy. My parents were so busy with their own lives they didn't spend a lot of time noticing my behavior or emotions.

At first it was just an occasional thing. I realized that the physical pain actually had some substance to it, and this helped me make sense of things. After a few months, things started getting out of control; I was sneaking around cutting myself using the different tools I had hidden.

I went to stay with my father for his birthday about six weeks after I had begun cutting. When I didn't bring a birthday card, my stepmom made a really big deal about it. I think this was my breaking point. I responded by trying to commit suicide and ended up in the kids unit of a psych ward. My youth pastor was with me when I went in. They asked me if I had been cutting myself. I could not lie to my youth pastor, so I told the truth. I had been carving my wrists by this time. I think I had wanted them to find out so that I could stop living a lie. This was when my family started to realize my problem was real.

I stopped cutting for about one month, but then I started again. I also decided to stop seeing my dad. I went for a year without seeing him. I stayed with my mom because I knew that I did better while I was staying with her. Even though my counselor encouraged me to contact my dad, I didn't.

In March of my junior year, things started to finally come around with my relationship with Dad. One day, out of the blue, my dad called and asked if I wanted to help him out with his work. I wasn't sure what to do: Did I want to work with my dad or keep avoiding him? I told my youth leader about the opportunity, and he encouraged me to take it. So I did, and it helped to heal my relationship with Dad.

I stopped cutting January of my sophomore year. I realized that hurting myself like that was just hurting *myself*—no one else. It was a daily battle to stop. I didn't have any friends who cut; I don't even know how I learned about it. But even now, when I go home for the holidays, it's like I know I have the option.

The process of learning how to cope with pain and stress has been an ongoing battle for me. Now, I run or ride my bike when I'm stressed out. I've also learned the necessity of making active decisions every day about how to deal with stress. I write a lot. I write out my feelings and process that way. Sometimes I write out my prayers to God. There are also a few people in my life, people I trust and who don't blame me for what happened, who I talk to. One specific person always says "I accept you," which means a lot to me. I need to know that someone will love and accept me no matter what happens. This motivates me to keep walking toward God.

People would tell me over and over that I needed to get over all of the pain from the past and live my life in the present. They'd often tell me that "time heals all wounds." I do not believe that this statement does justice to real feelings of pain. Years have passed since my pain started from my parent's divorce, but I experience this pain in some way almost every day. The good news is that each day I also am reminded of God's love for me. Life has dark detours, bumps, and lonely nights, but I see God's hands holding me and his power healing my scars.

Care and Counseling Tips

THE BASICS

When you discover that a student in your ministry is engaging in destructive behavior, such as eating disorders, self-injury, or dangerous games, your first instinct might be to panic. Sometimes you might observe physical indications that the student has been participating, such as scars or open wounds on his or her wrists. You may notice a pattern of weight loss that seems unexplainable. Or you might just hear self-deprecating comments that let you know the teenager is feeling critical of him or herself.

While all of these behaviors have the potential of being deadly, there are ways to prevent and intervene in these situations.

Care Tips

Understanding your student's actions and the possible underlying reasons for his or her choices is the first step in helping your student.

+ Eating Disorders

For a formal diagnosis of anorexia nervosa, a teenager must be refusing to maintain a body weight that is considered normal for his or her height. The student usually has an intense fear of gaining weight or becoming fat, even when the student is underweight. Teenagers with bulimia, on the other hand, don't usually actively refuse to maintain their normal weight. However, they will binge eat and then either purge the food from their bodies or compensate by fasting or engaging in excessive exercise.

What May Be Going On: Eating disorders often result from teenagers needing to feel an element of control over their circumstances. For example, a student whose home life seems out of control may see refusing to eat food as a way to make a choice for him or herself. No one can make the student eat, so that is one area over which he or she can make personal decisions. Body image also plays a critical role. Adolescents' bodies are changing rapidly, and they compare themselves with their peers.

+ Self-Injury

Teenagers who self-injure typically do so by cutting or burning. They can use many different objects, from knives or glass to erasers and cigarettes. As the cuts or burns heal, they leave scars. Cutting often begins on an impulse, but receiving attention for it can reinforce it.

What May Be Going On: Self-injury often provides a way for teenagers to release strong emotions they are feeling that they don't have other ways of getting out. When students experience overwhelming feelings, such as sadness, guilt, shame, anger, or fear, they need a way to express those emotions. If they haven't learned or chosen to use healthy skills—such as talking, exercising, or journaling—inflicting physical pain can seem like the only way to feel better. Sometimes self-injury involves a desire to kill oneself, but often it's just a cry for help.

+ Dangerous Games

A new trend among teenagers is engaging in dangerous games, such as playing Chicken with oncoming traffic or trains, or participating in the Choking Game—a game that involves using different methods to achieve unconsciousness. Sometimes other teenagers will put pressure on the person's carotid artery, restricting blood flow to the brain. Other times, a student will use a ligature and perform the strangulation on him or herself. This game can easily result in death, especially for teenagers who practice it alone and have no one to release the pressure of the ligature after becoming unconscious.

What May Be Going On: Dangerous games are often about peer pressure and lack of education. Most students have no idea how dangerous the game is, and developmentally they're at a stage where they believe nothing can hurt them. The games also make the student feel powerful and provide a "high," which can become addictive.

SCRIPTURE HELP

+ **Genesis 1:26-27**
+ **Psalm 118:5-9**
+ **Psalm 138:3**
+ **Isaiah 57:18-19**
+ **Luke 15:1-7**

+ **Romans 8:31-39**
+ **2 Corinthians 5:1-10**
+ **Philippians 4:13**
+ **Jude 17-23**
+ **Revelation 21:1-7**

Counseling Tips

+ Listen carefully.

There can be many underlying reasons for students to engage in destructive behaviors. Each student will have different experiences and different feelings. Taking time to really understand the student will help you figure out how to intervene and give the teenager a safe place to express him or herself.

+ Educate your students.

Continually discuss the subjects of body image, peer pressure, and expression of feelings in your ministry. Don't be afraid to bring up topics such as anorexia, cutting, and dangerous games. Start early and let teenagers know how destructive those behaviors can be.

You might consider having a guest speaker address your group about eating disorders, self-injury, or dangerous games in your weekly meeting. Or split the students into small groups and provide some discussion questions. Revisit these issues every few months so students will see your ministry as a safe place for dialogue.

+ Identify triggers.

Help your student figure out when he or she engages in the behaviors. Is it after interacting with a stressful relative? Is it a result of peer pressure? Is your student feeling isolated? Work with your teenager to avoid those situations in the future. Suggest having a friend call to check up after a stressful day at school or getting involved in an after-school activity to feel more connected to other teenagers.

+ Replace negative behaviors with positive ones.

Instead of playing the Choking Game to get an adrenaline rush, your student could get involved in martial arts or another activity that involves physical exertion. When your teenager is tempted to binge and purge, help him or her make a healthy menu decision and then take a walk after dinner. Instead of engaging in self-injury when emotional pain seems overwhelming, your student can hold an ice cube in his or her hand, which provides a feeling of discomfort without the danger of cutting. When trying to stop one behavior, it's most effective to replace it with a better choice.

+ Build trust.

Establish relationships with your students that will allow for open communication about destructive behaviors. When you express concern within this context, they'll listen.

WHEN TO REFER

Refer when you notice any of the following:

+ **Eating Disorders:** food-abusing behavior, dramatic weight loss, friendships disrupted by food abuse, a student who has a body image that is extremely distorted

+ **Self-Injury:** behavior that is accompanied by symptoms of depression or anxiety (see Chapter 2, "Depression," and Chapter 10, "Stress and Anxiety"), behavior that has caused severe injury, other factors that seem to be causing significant stress such as family conflict or academic struggles, a student who is unable to identify or choose healthy coping skills for stress and anxiety

+ **Dangerous Games:** a student who is continuing to engage in hazardous games after being educated about the dangers, a student who seems to be addicted to the "high" he or she experiences when playing, a student who is pressuring others to play

Group Tips

+ Have a team of responders.

Don't let only one person hold the responsibility of helping a group member who practices destructive behaviors. Share the load.

+ Encourage other-care as well as self-care.

Even hurting people can reach out to others. Plan community service events and encourage the self-destructive student to join in. Helping others can be a distraction from depression and isolation, and can make the hurting student feel good about contributing to something positive.

+ Remember that self-destructive behavior is an external sign of internal pain.

There's something inside that you can't see going on. Be aware that the problem is not just surface. It's deep and painful. Work to make your group environment the safe place. Don't let people gossip about one another, respond with loud shock, or condemn one another's choices. Work to become good listeners.

What Not to Say

+ "Oh, that's so gross!"

Starving oneself, throwing up, or self-induced cuts don't sound like terrific Friday-night activities to many people, but it's no reason to react instinctively to an admission of destructive behavior. Be calm. Listen.

+ "Yeah, I'd wondered if something was going on. You've been lookin' pretty bad lately."

Even if it's true, don't say it. It's not helpful to know they've been looking "pretty bad." But it will be helpful to know you're concerned and you care.

+ "I'd wondered who would be the unlucky percentage in our group."

Don't detach yourself emotionally to avoid personal interaction. Plus, it's never good to talk about statistics when someone is sharing pain.

What to Say

+ "Thank you for trusting me enough to talk to me."

Admitting self-destructive behavior is a big step and an even bigger admission of trust. Thank the student for that.

+ "I'm sad to see you hurting."

Express your concern and care for the student's physical state as well as for his or her spiritual and emotional state. Destructive behaviors are both internally and externally painful.

+ "God cares about your body."

It's one thing to say that God cares about someone's soul; it's something entirely different to say that God cares about someone's body. Remind students that God created them in his image and that one day, God will resurrect their bodies. The body is not simply a person's shell—God calls us to take care of ourselves.

ADDITIONAL RESOURCES

+ Books

How Did This Happen? A Practical Guide to Understanding Eating Disorders—for Teachers, Parents and Coaches. Minneapolis: Institute for Research and Education, HealthSystem Minnesota, 1999.

Secret Scars: Uncovering and Understanding the Addiction of Self-Injury. V. J. Turner. Center City, MN: Hazelden Foundation, 2002.

+ Online Resources

www.deadlygameschildrenplay.com/en/home.asp
(Deadly Games Children Play)

www.edap.org (National Eating Disorders Association)

CHAPTER TWELVE

Gender Identity and Sexual Choices
Equipping Students to Make Wise Sexual Choices

with counseling insights from
JULIE A. ODELL, M.A. AND
SCOTT GIBSON, M.S.W., L.C.S.W.
+ ministry tips from JOY-ELIZABETH F. LAWRENCE

In a mid-sized Midwestern city, Miss Cindy, a Christian social worker and later an urban youth pastor, started a small group she named GIRLS—an acronym for Girls In Real Life Situations. This name is dead-on.

When she was 12, Maggie joined GIRLS and participated in the conversation and activities. They discussed sex and relationships. She listened as Miss Cindy honestly described the baggage that results from sexual indiscretion.

Maggie's life has been hard. Her "real-life situation" includes an absent, alcoholic father. Though he was around when she was young, she doesn't know where he lives and hasn't seen him in over five years. He occasionally calls her, but she doesn't know him. Maggie also has a stubborn and independent temperament—a great resource in tough situations, but it often comes with an unwillingness to listen to and obey authority.

Despite Miss Cindy's discussions about sex and its consequences, Maggie started having sex at 15. The first time was completely unplanned; she was with her best friend's brother, and it just happened. She knew she wasn't in love. When she told Miss Cindy and the other members of GIRLS, she was honest. Miss Cindy asked, "Why did you do it?" Maggie responded, "Because I wanted to."

In the summer before her junior year, Maggie was raped.

The following fall, Maggie began a relationship with a boy she really liked. The couple cared about each other and had sex. Later that fall, the GIRLS group went on a mission trip to a city eight hours away. As soon as they arrived in the city, Maggie started complaining about feeling sick. First, she said it was her stomach. Then, she said it was her butt. Finally, she was specific. It was her genitals. Miss Cindy took Maggie to the hospital, where the doctors diagnosed her with herpes. Maggie spent the entire mission trip recovering from her first outbreak. She had contracted herpes from her rapist earlier that summer. She went on medication that she will have to take for the rest of her life.

Maggie remained stubborn and independent, but honest within the context of her group. She contracted chlamydia from another sexual partner. Other members of GIRLS made choices, too. Some became teen mothers. Others remained virgins. All stayed honest; it was their accountability group, after all. Maggie is adamant about the group's involvement in one another's lives. "We help each other out," she says, describing the way one will call the other for immediate help. Additionally, Maggie keenly describes how Miss Cindy first took the time to get to know the girls before speaking individually to each one about their sexual choices. "First, she was there for us," she says, "then, she was someone we could talk to." Miss Cindy has the ability to be nonplused by the girls' decisions; she doesn't get mad at them or yell. "But you can see the disappointment in her eyes," Maggie says. "Maybe it's just me, but I can see it."

Miss Cindy is passionate about her role in these girls' lives. She's honest with them about her choices, too, including her mistakes. Over and over she tells the girls, "You are a child of God." In describing sexual choices and God's boundaries for us, she tells a story about a backyard. "There was this father who loved his children so much," she says. "He had a giant backyard in which he put an Olympic-sized swimming pool, a terrific sandbox with all the toys you could ever want, a trampoline with bounce so great you could easily do triple flips. Around the yard he put a picket fence, about 2 feet high, to mark the backyard.

"His son was jumping on the trampoline. As he jumped, he noticed the neighbor's trampoline. It was red and looked terrific. *He* wanted a red trampoline. The daughter was playing in the sandbox. She looked up and saw a group of scary men walking by with a scary dog, growling at her. She was afraid of being in the backyard.

"The father was concerned that his children weren't enjoying his yard as he had intended them to. He had a great idea. He would build a brick wall, 10 feet tall, to keep his children from being afraid of or wanting what was on the other side. He put up the wall, and his children were happy with what their father had given them."

Miss Cindy explains how this is why God has given us sexual boundaries—to protect us from being afraid, to protect us from wanting what others have. Maggie agrees.

When asked how her experiences have influenced her choices today, Maggie can't help but talk about her 13-year-old sister, Lisa. Maggie hopes that by seeing her own choices, Lisa will make different ones. So far, she has. Lisa is still a virgin. She has seen Maggie bedridden for a week with herpes outbreaks. Maggie is so passionate about her influence on Lisa that she tears up and looks away when she begins talking about it. Lisa cares about Maggie, too—she doesn't want her to have a boyfriend. Maggie isn't currently dating anyone, and she tries to avoid being alone with boys her age. She hangs out in groups or with her mom to avoid temptation.

And the GIRLS group? They still meet, talk, and hold each other accountable. Even though Maggie is about to graduate from high school, she'll continue in the group—she's been in it for six years, after all.

Care and Counseling Tips

THE BASICS

With teenagers feeling pressure from peers and the media, adult role models, and the hormones in their changing bodies, you may be noticing inappropriate sexual behaviors cropping up in your youth group. Girls may be wearing provocative, revealing clothes to your events; you may overhear guys talking about women as sex objects. Both guys and girls may be questioning their sexuality and wondering if they might be homosexual.

Teenagers are attempting to discover who they are, what their role is in society, and what it means to be female or male. As they develop their social identity, they'll be confronted with questions concerning their gender identity (their sense of being male or female), their gender role (the behaviors, attitudes, and characteristics associated with each gender), and their sexual choices. Many factors have an impact on this development:

• Media Influence
Most teenagers are bombarded with inappropriate and unrealistic media images of "ideal" teenage appearance and behavior. The role models that many teenagers identify with are often overly sexualized and illustrate extreme sex-role stereotypes: Males are macho and muscular; females are a paradox, both seductive and sexually submissive.

• Adult Models
Teenagers observe the significant men and women in their lives and develop ideas about appropriate ways for each gender to behave. Families tend to have rules surrounding gender roles—spoken and unspoken, healthy and unhealthy.

• Changing Bodies
Adolescence is a period of major growth and change—physically,

emotionally, and cognitively. Because this change happens at a different rate for each teenager, your students may feel overwhelmed, confused, and self-conscious about their appearance.

SCRIPTURE HELP

+ **Genesis 2:18-25**
+ **Deuteronomy 26:16-19**
+ **John 8:1-11**
+ **John 10:10b**
+ **1 Corinthians 6:12-20**
+ **Ephesians 2:1-10**
+ **Ephesians 5:1-13**
+ **Colossians 3:1-17**
+ **1 Thessalonians 4:1-12**
+ **1 Peter 1:13-25**

WHEN TO REFER

The students you will want to refer for further counseling are in the following situations:
+ **Living a "double life"**
+ **Facing an unplanned pregnancy**
+ **Struggling with sexual identity or sexual preference issues**
+ **Involved in promiscuous sexual activity and putting themselves in high-risk situations**
+ **Reporting previous sexual abuse or assault**
+ **Feeling significantly distressed about their gender identity, appropriate gender role, or sexual choices**

Care Tips

When students come to you with questions about their gender identity or sexual choices, here are some things to keep in mind:

+ Be prepared.

Don't let tough questions like this catch you off guard. If you seem surprised or embarrassed by the subject, you will reinforce to the teenager that it's not OK to ask. Take a deep breath and remember that it took a lot of courage for the student to come to you.

+ Be understanding.

Often students feel isolated because they don't realize their experiences are normal. Your major task is to normalize the student's troublesome thoughts and feelings. You can do this by using simple statements such as "I've heard that your experiences are fairly common" or "I remember feeling like that when I was your age."

+ Be encouraging.

Many teenagers struggle with body image issues, which may be tied to their gender identity. Help students identify their negative beliefs about their bodies and replace them with positive thoughts.

+ Be open.

Teenagers may hide their experiences because of shame and fear of judgment and rejection. You want youth to feel able to approach you. Create a nonjudgmental and nonthreatening atmosphere in your youth group by being open to talk about touchy subjects. When subjects come up, don't first condemn—be willing to listen and talk, building a foundation of trust.

Counseling Tips

Gender and sex issues can be ongoing subjects in your ministry. Use these tips to help students form positive views of themselves and their sexuality:

+ Challenge stereotypes.

Teenagers may have general concerns about gender identity and wonder, "Am I masculine (or feminine) enough?" The answer to this question will depend to some extent on each student's concept and understanding of appropriate gender roles. You can facilitate a study on men or women in the Bible or on the characteristics of Jesus himself. The goal is to help students focus on God's perspective of masculinity and femininity, rather than on society's view.

+ Be attuned to normal sexual curiosity.

Adolescents need to figure out what to do with this new aspect of their life. Students will naturally be curious about new things, sex included. When they have the opportunity to explore, discuss, and learn about their sexuality in safe ways, they will be better equipped to honor God in their sexual decisions.

Try dedicating a youth meeting to the topic, "What the Bible Says About Sex (and What It Doesn't)." Before that meeting, invite parents to a separate forum so they'll understand what you'll be communicating as well as how they can help their teenagers have healthy, God-honoring relationships.

+ Encourage abstinence.

Don't give up teaching your students to wait to have sex until marriage. Even though they receive many other messages from their peers and the media, they will look to you for guidance about how to stay pure. Equate sex to marriage and give the subject of sex the fortitude it deserves. If you send them this consistent message and have established yourself as a trusting adult role model, your students will remember your advice when they are in emotionally charged situations.

ADDITIONAL RESOURCES

+ Books

Passport to Purity. Dennis and Barbara Rainey. Little Rock, AR: FamilyLife, 1999.

Someone Like Me: A Youth Devotional on Identity. Annette LaPlaca. Colorado Springs, CO: WaterBrook Press, 2001.

So What Does God Have to Do With Who I Am? Joey O'Connor. Grand Rapids, MI: Fleming H. Revell Co., 2001.

+ Online Resources

www.freetobeme.com (New Direction for Life Ministries)

HOMOSEXUALITY

What should you do if a student in your ministry confides in you that he or she feels homosexual tendencies? First, don't overreact. Talk to the student about what feelings the student is experiencing and what beliefs he or she has about sexuality. Second, explain to the student that curiosity about different sexual experiences is normal. See if you can answer questions about sexuality the student may have. Finally, keep the door open for continued nonjudgmental conversation with the student. Sexual development is a journey that happens over a lifetime, not a single event that occurs in adolescence.

Group Tips

+ Don't make one sexual sin worse than another.

Some groups will embrace women who are pregnant outside of marriage with grace and mercy, but when a student begins questioning his or her sexual orientation, they turn coldly away. Embrace all people in your group, and reject all sin equally.

+ Don't give up or change your expectations and standards.

Keep sexual purity a top priority. Don't lower it, even if no one is sexually pure. Keep encouraging one another. It is a lie to believe that people who are sexually impure can't change. They can, with God's help.

+ Start young.

Start talking about sexual choices at a young age. Youth are going to hear about sexual choices somewhere, and it may as well be within the context of a Christian community. Also, talk to your students about their role models and the media messages they experience.

+ Don't gossip.

If you suspect a student is involved in a sexual relationship, go directly to the student. Don't speak to the student's parents. Don't ask his or her friends. Go to the source and ask gently.

What Not to Say

+ "Was it good?"
Don't joke around when a student tells you about his or her sexual choices. There's enough of that at school and work.

+ "You're a slut."
One mother, on learning that her daughter was sexually active, called her "Jezebel" and the "whore of Satan." Name-calling is never appropriate, even when it's true.

+ "Well, you know what the Bible says about purity..."
Sure, the Bible says a lot about sexual purity and choices. However, pointing this out is probably not the first thing you should do. Many students will be struggling with shame, and it probably took a lot of courage to approach you. A student may fear your initial reaction will be judgment. Build trust by first listening and understanding. In some situations, a discussion about biblical sexual mandates is important. Other times, a student may be well-versed in God's sexual standards and simply need someone to listen, understand, and advise.

What to Say

+ "Did you plan this or was it something you decided in the moment?"
Sometimes people plan sexual behavior beforehand. Other times, they go with the flow and end up naked in bed. This question can lead to important discussions about *why* we engage in sinful sexual activity and how our small choices can lead to big consequences.

+ "What are you missing in your life?"

We all try to fill the void. Sometimes the void may be a parent's love. It may be physical or economic needs. It may be loneliness or depression. This question is a good conversation opener.

+ "You are God's child."

Everyone needs to be reminded of his or her identity and value in Christ. God didn't give us sexual mandates because he's a spoilsport. God gave us boundaries to protect our hearts—and our bodies.

+ "What will you do differently next time?"

Students must have sexual standards in order to make wise choices. Standards may include "I will keep all my clothes on all the time" or "I will not be in my room or a car alone with a guy."

+ "God made you in his image."

Christianity is a religion that's all about the human body—so much so, in fact, that we believe in the resurrection of the body. That says something about God's value of the human person-body. In the Christian faith, people's bodies are valuable. Teach the significance of the body and how we should use it.

Notes

Notes

Notes

_____
_____
_____
_____
_____
_____
_____
_____
_____
_____
_____
_____
_____
_____
_____
_____
_____
_____
_____
_____
_____
_____

Notes

_____

_____

_____

_____

_____

_____

_____

_____

_____

_____

_____

_____

_____

_____

_____

_____

_____

_____

_____

For more **amazing resources**

visit us at
www.group.com...

...or call us at
1-800-747-6060 ext. 1370!

Incredible things will happen™